Additional Praise for
The Baptist Health Care Journey to Excellence

"This book is a WOW! After years of pacesetting headlines and tantalizing fragments, the whole Baptist story has finally been told in captivating detail. A new Mecca for hospital leaders has emerged as the healthcare example of world-class culture. Their story cannot be ignored and will become the blueprint for many other organizations to go from good to great."

—Fred Lee
Author of *If Disney Ran Your Hospital,*
9 Things You Would Do Differently

"The Story of Baptist Health Care to achieve workforce and service excellence is uncommon among healthcare giving organizations. It shouldn't be. The devotion of the Baptist leadership to create and sustain excellence out of once average and even mediocre performance is enlightening to all committed to service excellence and to enabling workers to, with pride, achieve their highest possible performance. For those who continue to find this elusive, this book, this story is for you."

—Joel H. Ettinger
Pugh Ettinger McCarthy Associates

"Al Stubblefield presents an inspiring story that shouts out to us that a culture can be changed for the better! Then he gives us the nuts and bolts that let us get started and stop making excuses."
—Andy Andrews
Author of the New York Times Best-Seller,
The Traveler's Gift

"The human aspects of the workplace deserve renewed attention in all organizations today. Stubblefield masterfully gives a roadmap for cultural change that results in trust, pride, and productivity. The Baptist Health Care story shows any industry step by step how to achieve better results."

—Barbara Pagano, Ed.S.
Co author, *The Transparency Edge:*
How Credibility Can Make or Break You in Business.
Selected as *Fast Company's* Book of the Month for March 2004.

"Non-fiction, but captivating as a novel. Educational, inspirational. Should be required reading for every leader driven to improve organizational culture and performance."
—Roger E. Herman,
Author, *How to Become an Employer of Choice*

"There is a well documented 'quality chasm' in America crying out for the need to do things differently. Al Stubblefield aptly describes Baptist Health Care Systems' remarkable journey in winning the Baldrige Award. It demonstrates that it *is* possible to change cultures, implement sustainable improvements in service delivery, and empower all working for the patient to continuously improve. There are practical lessons here and great inspirations for everyone on the quality improvement journey."

—Stephen M. Shortell, Ph.D., M.P.H.
Dean and Blue Cross of California
Distinguished Professor of Health Policy Management
University of California, Berkeley

"WOW! This is much more than a description of the Baptist journey to Excellence. It is a clear roadmap for real leaders who truly want to transform their organizations to Excellence and beyond."

—Jamie Orlikoff,
President, Orlikoff & Associates, Inc.
Executive Director, American Governance & Leadership Group

"As with all great leaders who write accurate histories of how their organizations succeeded, you'll find very little about Al Stubblefield in this book. As I read it, I noticed how many times he used the words 'we' and not 'I'—a clear sign of how he views the world of excellence he initiated and helped create. What you will find is almost a 'journal' on the real-world transformation of Baptist Health Care into a premier, trend setting organization—started because Al was willing to jolt himself and others out of old assumptions and certainties, lead by example rather than words, and invite everyone who would listen out of intellectual and emotional pollution and into the fresh air of letting the best ideas wins."

—Steve Smith
Co-author, *businessThink*

"Wow! Al Stubblefield has demonstrated transformational leadership. He rallied his entire team around a shared vision. He was relentless and unwavering in his quest. The success is obvious. The winners are employees, physicians, volunteers, and the patients and families served. Dedicated leadership does make a difference."

—Jim Nathan
CEO, Lee Memorial Health System

"In this book Al Stubblefield provides a step-by-step guide to how an uncompromising commitment to service excellence, employee empowerment and development, and measurement and accountability can lead to a cultural transformation for healthcare organizations that want to survive and thrive in an industry confronting irreconcilable demographic, technological, financial and service delivery challenges. Baptist Health Care's journey from mediocrity to winning the coveted Malcolm Baldrige National Quality Award is a journey to excellence other healthcare organizations can and should follow."

—Ed Ranelli
Dean, College of Business
University of West Florida

"Al Stubblefield knows from experience what it really takes to transform an organization to create superlative performance. Al's lively and informative exposition of the Baptist Health Care story and the stories of many others, not only gives us the inspiration to make our healthcare organizations work better, but also provides the practical advice to help make deep, lasting, and profound cultural change."

—Ian Morrison, Health Care Futurist and Author,
Healthcare in the New Millennium: Vision, Values, and Leadership

"Journey to Excellence is a story of a cultural revolution in healthcare! In 1995, Baptist Health Care faced the brutal facts of their environment and decided to take their mission statement off the wall. They began to walk the talk. While some leaders and some organizations talk of change, the Baptist team focused on execution, they focused on action. This book is a must-read for all interested in the nuts and bolts of change that leads to competitive advantage and to improved delivery of healthcare. This is not a history lesson; the Baptist team continues their journey today.

—Melvin F. Hall, Ph.D.
President & CEO Press Ganey Associates

THE
BAPTIST
HEALTH CARE
JOURNEY TO
EXCELLENCE

*Creating a Culture
That WOWs!*

AL STUBBLEFIELD

WILEY

JOHN WILEY & SONS, INC.

Published by John Wiley & Sons, Inc., Hoboken, New Jersey.
Published simultaneously in Canada.

For general information on our other products and services, or technical support, please contact our Customer Care Department within the United States at 800-762-2974, outside the United States at 317-572-3993 or fax 317-572-4002.

Wiley also publishes its books in a variety of electronic formats. Some content that appears in print may not be available in electronic books.

For more information about Wiley products, visit our Web site at *www.wiley.com*.

Library of Congress Cataloging-in-Publication Data:

Stubblefield, Al.
  The Baptist health care journey to excellence : creating a culture that WOWs! / Al Stubblefield.
     p. cm.
  Includes index.
  ISBN 0-471-70890-9 (cloth)
  1. Health services administration—United States. 2. Health facilities—United States—Administration. 3. Medical care—Religious aspects—Christianity. I. Title.
  RA971.S86 2005
  362.1'0973—dc22
2004016892

Printed in the United States of America

10 9 8 7 6 5 4 3 2

Contents

**KEY FOUR   CONTINUOUSLY DEVELOP
GREAT LEADERS**

**KEY FIVE   HARDWIRE SUCCESS THROUGH
SYSTEMS OF ACCOUNTABILITY**

About the Author

Al Stubblefield is president and CEO of Baptist Health Care Corporation. In his current position since 1999, Mr. Stubblefield has been with the Baptist Health Care system from 1985 to the present. Before coming to Baptist Hospital, he worked in hospitals in Mississippi and Tennessee. Mr. Stubblefield currently serves on the American Hospital Association Board of Directors and is Chairman of the Regional Policy Board 4. He also serves on the Board of VHA Southeast and the Health Research and Education Trust.

In 2002, *Training Magazine* included Mr. Stubblefield as one of eleven "CEOs Who Get It," CEOs whose committment to workforce development sets them and their organizations apart. Also listed in the 2004 Modern Healthcare's annual ranking of the 100 Most Powerful People in Health Care, Mr. Stubblefield has become a frequent speaker at national conferences. Mr. Stubblefield delivers an inspiring message on the importance of culture development and employee engagement from a CEO's perspective.

Mr. Stubblefield is a Fellow of the American College of Healthcare Executives and has served on the board of Florida Hospital Association. He received a master of science degree from the University of Alabama in Birmingham, Alabama. He earned his bachelor's degree from Mississippi College in Clinton, Mississippi.

Mr. Stubblefield has been married for 29 years to Mary Lee and has four children, one son-in-law, and a granddaughter, who was born during the writing of this book.

ABOUT BAPTIST HEALTH CARE

On October 17, 2001, the 50th anniversary of the organization that has become Baptist Health Care Corporation was celebrated.

Fifty years ago Baptist Hospital was opened, a dream realized for a number of selfless community leaders who persevered, through 11 difficult years, to build a not-for-profit health care organization deeply committed to serving the needs of residents of Northwest Florida and South Alabama.

From the beginning, this organization formed a culture based on Christian values and principles and a passion for service excellence. The cornerstone for Baptist Hospital dedicates its facilities, "To the glory of God and the ministry of healing."

The culture at Baptist Health Care is truly unique. It is entrusted to improve the health and well being of the communities it serves, and lives its mission, values, and vision in all that it does. Its service is guided by five pillars of excellence: People, Service, Quality, Finance, and Growth.

The largest provider of health services in Northwest Florida, Baptist Health Care is a network of hospitals, nursing homes, mental health facilities, and outpatient centers. Serving Escambia and Santa Rosa counties in Florida and Escambia county in Alabama, Baptist Health Care also operates the Baptist LifeFlight helicopter ambulances. With more than 5,500 people on its payroll, Baptist Health Care is the largest locally-owned employer in the area.

Foreword

Impact. It's something that all of us eventually yearn for in life. The ability to influence the lives of others in a positive way.

While some professions seem naturally more inclined toward impact than others (police, firefighters, doctors, and clergy come to mind), managers of organizations all too often underestimate the influence they can have.

Al Stubblefield's WOW is many things, but at its heart, it is a testament to the power of leadership and teamwork and the impact that the manager of a healthy organization can have on the lives of people. In a manner that is at once simple, humble, and powerful, he tells the unbelievably true story of how a mediocre organization transformed itself into an extraordinary one.

But to be fair, Baptist Health Care was less than a mediocre organization before the transformation. And to be fair again, BHC has become more than an extraordinary company; it is a model for our time.

By combining lofty ideology with practical tools, Al paints a vivid picture of just how beautiful an organization's culture can be, and how it can ennoble the lives of its customers, employees, leaders, and community members alike.

But this book goes one step further; it impacts readers too. After reading WOW, I was touched by something far greater and deeper than business insight and leadership advice. I somehow felt proud of what has been accomplished at BHC, as though I were part of the organization myself! I felt a sense of joy for the patients and employees of BHC, and for their family and friends, all of whom have been touched by this cultural transformation. And perhaps most important of all, I now feel inspired to help other organizations understand the kind of impact they can have by undertaking a similar transformation.

I encourage anyone reading this book to do so with a notebook and pen handy, because the lessons contained are practical and abundant. I hope that you can extract every available nugget of wisdom from it, and that it impacts your culture profoundly. And I hope that you feel as touched as I did by what an otherwise ordinary group of men and women in Pensacola, Florida did to make the world a better place.

Patrick Lencioni
Author, *The Five Dysfunctions of a Team*

Acknowledgments

How do you acknowledge the work of thousands of coworkers? These wonderful people helped craft a powerful vision, and then, by golly, set out and made it happen. They have given me a story to tell and I hope I have done it justice. In 2001, when we received notice that we had earned a site visit (the only healthcare organization to make it that year) for the Malcolm Baldrige National Quality Award, I thanked Joel Ettinger who had consulted with us in putting together our application. Joel's humble reply was "I just helped you tell the story in Baldrige language. The story and the results were there." That is the way I feel about this book. The story is there, being lived out every day by a group of workers that feel and act like they own the joint, refuse to make excuses, and just keep raising the bar higher and higher for themselves and for hundreds of thousands of healthcare workers nationwide. Leading you is truly a privilege and I thank you for giving me such an incredible story to tell.

When Pam Bilbrey came to me and suggested that we put the story of our journey into a book and that she thought I should write it, I said, "let's do it." However, as with almost everything I have gotten credit for in my life, this work is the product of dozens upon dozens of contributions from coworkers, family, and advisors. The first thanks goes to my coworkers that created the story. From there, Ken Shelton got us started and was a constant encourager and priceless advisor. The real savior for me in hitting our deadlines and making a living, breathing book out of a ton of great material was my daughter Beth. Beth agreed on the first of April to do what it took to meet our deadline of June 16th to have our book to the publisher. The only trick was that Beth had another commitment—to deliver our first grandchild on or about June 12th. The race was on. On June 11th at 5 PM we put the final wrap on this project, she took the 12th off and at 8:18 PM on the 13th made me a granddad. Is that good planning or what?

The rest of my family played significant roles, editing, typing, even reading chapters out loud as we drove to Gran and Grandmother's houses in Mississippi. My precious wife Mary Lee did what she always does best, which was to keep us all constantly lifted up in prayer (and making sure we ate our vegetables!!).

Coworkers made countless invaluable contributions in bringing this story to you. First and foremost, they made it happen so that there was a story to tell! Second, they edited, suggested stories, gave great input, prepared draft sections, gave honest feedback (ouch), and helped keep BHC and its mission and vision squarely in focus while I was distracted with this project. I hesitate to mention names, but must acknowledge special effort by David Sjoberg, Lynda Barrett, Craig Miller, and Barry Arnold. Two friends that provided great inspiration and invaluable advice along the way were Jim Harris and Richard Hill. Finally, I must especially thank Pam Bilbrey for her insights into what parts of the story needed to be told and how to organize them in a way that works.

We-my family, my coworkers, and I hope and pray that our story will help in some small way to improve the quality of life for patients and communities served by healthcare workers who really do passionately want to be a part of an organization that is sold out to service. We also are bold enough to believe that those simple yet profound principles can bring similar results far outside of healthcare. Try it—you'll be glad you did!!

Introduction:
From Ouch! to WOW!

I am a most fortunate man. I have spent the past 20 years working in an organization that has achieved some phenomenal results. For three consecutive years, Baptist Health Care has been ranked as one of *Fortune* magazine's Top 100 Organizations to Work for in America. All five of Baptist Health Care's hospitals have spent multiple years in the top one percent in patient satisfaction based on survey results from the largest hospital patient database in the world. This year, we were awarded the coveted Malcolm Baldrige National Quality Award by the President of the United States.

In these trying times for the health care industry, and in our incredibly competitive market, how we have achieved these WOW! results in such a short time is a fascinating story.

For the purposes of this book, the story starts in 1995 with an organization headed in the wrong direction. In the fourth quarter of that year, our patient satisfaction rating had reached an all-time low. We were devastated to learn that we had scored in the 18th percentile in patient satisfaction as compared to our peers. Earlier that year we had jumped on the reengineering bandwagon that swept across American business, and in doing so greatly damaged employee morale. We were also just ending five years of major merger discussions with three different organizations—another morale killer. While we may have had some legitimate excuses to hide behind, the bottom line was this: Our employees were unhappy, and unhappy employees lead to unhappy customers.

We conducted an attitude survey among our employees, and they made it abundantly clear that they were not pleased with the Baptist Health Care experience. In 13 of the 18 categories, our employees' attitudes about their workplace were negative. At the bottom of the list, eight deviations *below* the norm for the industry, was our employees' opinion of top management. We said, "Ouch!" All of us in management felt that pain.

In addition to severe internal problems, we also faced fierce competition in our marketplace. Our flagship, Baptist Hospital, is in the worst location of three hospitals in what probably should be a two-hospital metro area. *Modern Healthcare* magazine recognized the competitiveness of our market several years ago when they included Pensacola as one of the top ten most competitive health care markets in the country. Both of our major competitors are owned by national healthcare conglomerates, and outspending them on facilities and equipment has always been out of the question. Their pockets are simply much deeper than ours.

So, in those dark days, we asked ourselves: Do we stop trying? Do we merge with one of our competitors, hand them the keys, and no longer have a community-owned healthcare system?

I would imagine that some of you may have asked similar questions. Anyone in a position of organizational leadership or ownership who faces tough competition and opposition may consider giving up during difficult days.

My answer, echoed by our entire management team, was simple, yet resolute: Not just yet. We're not willing to concede defeat. We think we can compete, but with a new premise—no longer Ouch!, but WOW!

It is my pleasure and privilege to recount the details of our amazing turnaround—the story of a cultural revolution that has been executed by the 5,500 employees of Baptist Health Care, even as they continue to make it happen. As COO and then CEO of this wonderful organization, I have had the advantage of seeing this transformation firsthand. I have observed it, I have played a role in it, and I have marveled at what has been achieved by the incredible team of people with whom I have had the privilege to work. It's a great story, and it has been—and continues to be—the most rewarding experience of my professional career.

PAIN PROMPTS CHANGE

The cold, hard fact of tough competition prompted us to start this journey, this quest for excellence. The following premise has always been true in life, as in business: *Pain prompts change.* Pain has a way of getting your attention. When you find yourself in a condition of acute or chronic pain, you want one thing above all else—relief. You discover that you are willing to make changes, even drastic ones, if they offer that hope.

As a healthcare corporation, you might say we are in the pain-prevention and abatement business. Many people come to us and become our customers because they are in pain. They want relief, and they want to return to their families and their lives. They seek our services—and those of our physicians—because they hope to feel better and regain a state of health and vigor as quickly as possible.

But here's the rub: People in pain have a better chance of getting well if treated in a healthy culture. In 1995, before our turnaround began, we were asking our employees to make sick people well, but we were expecting them to do it in an unhealthy culture. We took an important step toward transformation when we recognized that our workers would never perform at the highest level until we made them happy about being at work. In other words, we needed a culture change.

The story of that cultural transformation is the story I want to tell in this book. It is a story of leaders who have been willing to make painful adjustments in their leadership styles, of employees who have wholeheartedly bought into our culture and truly made things happen, and of workers at every level of the organization joining together to create an environment where people can find healing as quickly and effectively as possible.

I know it goes against the grain of the stereotypical workplace. It may even seem counterintuitive, but this is my experience:

People can be as healthy and happy at work as they are at home, or even more so.

At Baptist Health Care, we have established a workplace culture where our employees find satisfaction in their jobs and in turn create a healing environment for the customers and patients we serve. This type of transformation has only been made possible as we have become a WOW! workplace, empowering our *W*orkers to become *O*wners and *W*inners. That is our secret.

As I share the details of this amazing journey with you, I hope you will find my insights and suggestions applicable to your situation. Whether your organization is continuing its journey toward excellence or striking out in a new direction, may this book empower you to create a WOW! environment in your own workplace.

—Al Stubblefield
CEO of Baptist Health Care
Pensacola, Florida
October 2004

CHAPTER 1

In Search of Competitive Advantage

Competition is a painful thing, but it produces great results.
—Jerry Flint, in *Forbes Magazine*

J ust as our amazing turnaround has not happened overnight, neither did our descent to such dismal satisfaction ratings occur quickly. A variety of factors contributed to our downturn, including poor management decisions, changes in the healthcare industry, and other distracting pursuits that ultimately proved more harmful than beneficial. These factors, combined with lack of vision, caused us to lose our focus as a healthcare organization.

We had meandered into the last decade of the twentieth century, maintaining our status, as I like to put it, as an "outstanding mediocre hospital system." We were doing okay, although our accomplishments were not especially noteworthy. With the unique challenges that the next few years brought, however, our status, even as "mediocre," came into question.

I often refer to the period of the early 1990s as "Merger Mania." The "bigger is better" philosophy reigned in the business world, and the healthcare sector eagerly bought into that ideology. We at Baptist Health Care became convinced, along with most in our industry, that we needed to form partnerships with other companies to create larger and stronger organizations if we were going to survive. We began seeking potential partners as we attempted to prepare ourselves for the future of healthcare.

Our leadership team spent about five years in major merger discussions. We looked at three potential partners and held untold numbers of strategy meetings with board members and the senior management team. We met frequently with staff from the other organizations, calculating the potential savings of merging information systems and dreaming of increased negotiating strength and purchasing power. However, all three times, our grand plans fell through, and we found ourselves back at the drawing board.

Although none of these talks led to a deal, merger mania affected us on the local level as well. While we had been busy pursuing various state- and regionwide ventures, we had also been actively expanding our local presence by both acquisition and innovation. By 1995, we had successfully added a large community mental health center to our organization, affiliated with two area rural hospitals, and started building a physician company. In three years we had grown from 2,300 employees to over 5,000.

Finally in 1995, after five years of looking off into the distance, our leadership team began to turn its focus toward home. Baptist Health Care was growing; however, we had taken our eye off the ball. The disconcerting survey data that we were receiving was telling us that we had lost sight of our mission. Employees were unhappy with senior management, patient satisfaction was plummeting, and overall morale across the healthcare system was low. Clearly, we had become so obsessed with what was going on outside of the organization that we had forgotten to pay attention to the people on the inside. We had allowed Baptist Health Care to stray from its roots, evolving into an organization that was not performing up to its potential and was not satisfying its employees, not to mention its customers.

As this reality sank in, we began to see that in order to survive, we were going to have to make some dramatic changes. While we had not yet fully identified our problem, much less found the right solution, we were taking our first steps toward improvement. We had acknowledged that things had to change, and we were ready to do what it took to better our organization.

FINDING A COMPETITIVE EDGE

Before we could begin moving toward the change we sought, we needed to assess our present condition. An evaluation of our current position in the market identified some major challenges. Our two local competitors were hospitals owned, respectively, by the Daughters of Charity, an organization whose $2 billion war chest led the *Wall Street Journal* to call them "the Daughters of Currency," and the Hospital Corporation of America, an organization with immense equity capital. One of these local systems was at that time making a $300 million enhancement to their Pensacola campus, while the other was in the heyday of its equity accumulation. We were clearly at a financial disadvantage.

We recognized that we could not compete by out-spending our competitors on technology, facilities, or programs. Even if we had possessed the financial means to do so, those things were too easily duplicated, imitated, or outdone by competing organizations. So we asked ourselves: "How can we build a sustainable competitive advantage in our marketplace?" This question became even more critical when we considered that our main hospital facility, Baptist Hospital, was losing market share among insured and paying patients while its share of patients unable to pay for the care they received continued to grow. We began to see that even being as good as our competitors was not going to be enough. In order to survive, we were going to have to be noticeably better than the competition. But we still didn't know how to get there.

As we were asking these questions and searching desperately for a way to compete, a new ideological wave was sweeping American business. In what looked to us like just another business fad, consultants for Continuous Quality Improvement (CQI) encouraged corporations to strategically focus their efforts on improving quality and service. Not to be left out, we bought into these ideas, although somewhat halfheartedly, hiring a CQI consultant, and establishing a Quality Committee of our board of directors.

Robin Herr, a local plant manager for Armstrong World Industries and member of our board, was named chair of our quality committee. In meeting after meeting he would take the floor and emphatically announce, "Quality can be a competitive advantage!" I remember nodding politely, all the while thinking, "He doesn't know health care. You can't measure quality in health care." I wasn't sure what the answer to our problems was, but I was sure that it could be found in something much more concrete and measurable than "quality."

Eventually, though, we ran out of other options. We had already eliminated programs, facilities, equipment, and location as potential competitive advantages. What was left? As we continued to hear the quality message preached to us from a variety of sources, I began to wonder if maybe Robin Herr was right. Perhaps quality was an area where we could shine. I was also strongly encouraged by Jim Vickery, the President/CEO and my boss and mentor at the time, to grab hold of this "quality stuff" and make it work for Baptist Health Care.

If quality and service were truly going to be our competitive advantage, I knew that we would have to be able to measure them. Change happens much more slowly (or not at all) if you fail to keep track of where you've been and how far you've come. When we examined our current assessment tools, we found that we did have at least one instrument already in place to measure quality—our quarterly patient satisfaction surveys. These surveys measured how we rated against our peers in the area of customer service, an important quality indicator in healthcare.

So we decided that we could start there, with a new, strategic focus on *service excellence*. We said, "Let's build a service culture that will be very difficult to duplicate or compete with." We pledged that we would outperform our competitors by providing a level of service that our community—and even our nation—had never experienced before.

And that is how the turnaround began. Our organization reached a crucial turning point on the day that we committed to providing the highest level of customer service possible. While it may have gone unspoken at the time, that commitment to service excellence included a willingness to make the difficult changes necessary to get there. We knew we had a long road ahead, but we were ready to start moving in the right direction.

While turning our focus to service excellence may sound like a noble endeavor, it was born largely out of desperation. In effect, we heeded the sage advice of author and consultant Peter Drucker: "You don't have to change—survival is optional." We knew that without drastic changes, we would not survive; thus, creating a culture committed to service excellence was no less than a survival strategy. We saw no other option. In hindsight, I am convinced that there was no better option; service excellence should have been our focus from the beginning.

Another fortuitous part of this puzzle fell into place just as we began this journey eight years ago. Around that time, I began the transition into a role that better fit my management style. Jim Vickery, who was just the second CEO in the forty-eight-year history of Baptist Health Care, asked me to assume the role of Chief Operating Officer (COO) as he began to anticipate retirement.

I say this new role fit my style because I reveled in numbers and believed that objective survey data had the power to drive improvement. So, as COO, I began to look even more closely at the customer service measures that we already had in place. At the time, you had to have a strong stomach to digest the data we were getting. Our patient satisfaction scores in the eighteenth percentile meant that eighty-two percent of the hospitals in the survey were doing a better job of pleasing their customers than we were.

There was certainly room for improvement, and we believed that we might have found the key to turning those scores around. We had become convinced that an intense, unwavering focus on excellence in customer service would give us the competitive advantage we were so desperately seeking. Now the question was, "How do we get there?"

FOCUS ON EXCELLENCE

In October 1995, I walked into our board meeting and promised that we would raise our patient satisfaction scores from the eighteenth percentile in patient satisfaction to the seventy-fifth percentile *in nine months.* This was a radical but (I hoped!) achievable goal, and I believed that creating some quick wins was crucial to our success

When I walked out of the room after making that announcement, one of my senior officers took me aside and said, "Do you realize what you just did in there? You set us up for failure!"

Part of my reason for sharing this is that nine months later, when we had not only reached the seventy-fifth percentile but surpassed it, that officer was no longer with the organization. He and a handful of others who were unwilling to completely embrace our new culture had to be replaced. Those who remained, however, experienced the satisfaction of achieving that first challenging goal, and it only made them hungry for more.

How did we achieve such a tremendous turnaround so quickly? We discovered that the key to patient satisfaction is to focus not on patients first, but on your employees. We quickly realized that the satisfaction of our patients was directly related to the satisfaction of our employees; only happy, fulfilled employees will provide the highest level of healthcare to our patients. Therefore, we reasoned, "all" we had to do was find a way to satisfy every employee, who would then in turn create happy customers. With that determination, we faced an even harder question: How do we fill our organization with satisfied employees?

Every aspect of an employee's job, from compensation and benefits to management and supervision to reward and recognition, affects his or her overall job satisfaction. Therefore, an environment that breeds satisfied employees must be satisfying in every area. We were beginning to see that employee satisfaction was an all-encompassing goal. We were not going to find a quick fix; what we needed was genuine, "from the ground up" culture change.

The "aha" moment for me came when I recognized that all the deals we might make, all the joint ventures and all the mergers, and all the improvements in our financial position wouldn't mean much if our employees were miserable. We had to make our hospital a place where they were happy to be and happy to serve, and that would only be possible through a radical, thorough cultural transformation. True transformation would require a commitment from all of us. Creating a culture built on service excellence would demand some painful adjustments in our leaders and in our organization; every individual from the mailroom to the board room would have to wholeheartedly embrace our new cultural ideals. We knew that this kind of radical shift would never happen without a great deal of hard work, but we believed that the end result would be worth the effort that it took to get there.

Today, I can testify that creating an environment where employees are empowered to perform at the highest level has resulted in more than an inspired workforce. It has resulted in customer satisfaction ratings that are consistently in the ninety-ninth percentile—the best in the industry. Not surprisingly, these ratings have earned us considerable recognition.

Nearly all of Baptist Health Care's affiliated organizations use the Press, Ganey and Associates survey, the largest such database in America, to measure patient satisfaction. Incredibly, our Gulf Breeze Hospital has ranked number one in inpatient satisfaction for eight consecutive years. Gulf Breeze Hospital's Emergency Department has ranked first in its category for over three years. Inpatient scores for our affiliates Atmore Community Hospital, D. W. McMillan Hospital, and Jay Hospital combined have ranked second for most of the last five years. Our Baptist LifeFlight air ambulance service has had the top score for air ambulance programs for over two years. Scores for our comprehensive outpatient facility, Baptist Medical Park, have been in the top one percent since its doors opened three years ago. In 2004, Baptist's affiliated behavioral health services provider, Lakeview Center, was named number one in customer satisfaction by Mental Health Corporation of America for the fourth straight year (see Figure 1.1).

I remind you that we began this quest for performance excellence not because we wanted to gain national recognition, but because we wanted to survive. We believed that in order to compete in our market, we had to

FIGURE 1.1 Top One Percent in Patient Satisfaction

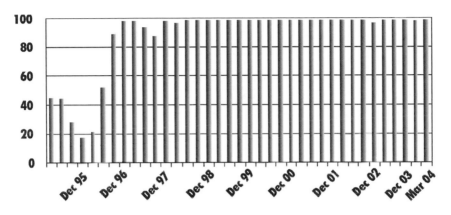

discernibly differentiate our services from the competition. The results of these efforts have surprised even us, and they are not limited to customer satisfaction scores; our finances have been affected as well. In a Baptist Health Care system review in June 1998, Moody's Investors Service noted that "investments in management training and cultural awareness are now beginning to generate favorable results in terms of new revenue and patient volume." Over a five-year period, we experienced an increase of nearly five percent in market share.

How have we achieved and maintained such amazing levels of patient satisfaction? By discovering we will never have satisfied customers without an engaged, motivated, and satisfied workforce. In the Introduction to this book, I referred to the poor results we received on our employee satisfaction survey in 1996. In that survey, across eighteen categories, our employees ranked us below the norm in thirteen areas, with an extremely low view of top management.

As we learned to support and empower our employees in ways that they could recognize and appreciate, they responded even more positively than we could have hoped. Eighteen months after receiving those disheartening employee satisfaction scores, we repeated the same survey. This time, employees rated Baptist Health Care above the norm in seventeen out of eighteen areas. When those results came in, we were told by the consultants who performed the survey for us that they had never before witnessed such dramatic improvement. Two years later, when they conducted the survey again, they told us they had never measured employee morale as high as ours in *any* organization, *anywhere*!

FIGURE 1.2a Employee Satisfaction Survey Results.
(Deviations from Norm)

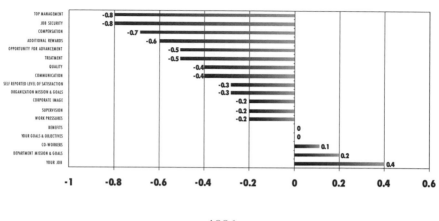

1996

We performed the survey again in 2001, after undergoing a significant transition in our hospital's senior management team. Although we expected our scores to slip back slightly after the transition, to our surprise they actually continued to rise. In 2003, they climbed even higher. Baptist

FIGURE 1.2c Employee Satisfaction Survey Results.
(Deviations from Norm)

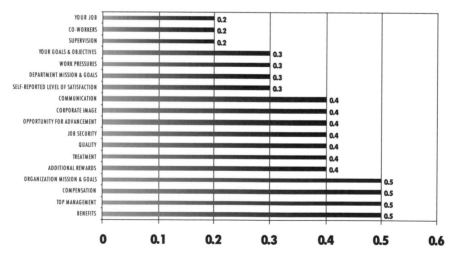

2001

FIGURE 1.2b Employee Satisfaction Survey Results.
                (Deviations from Norm)

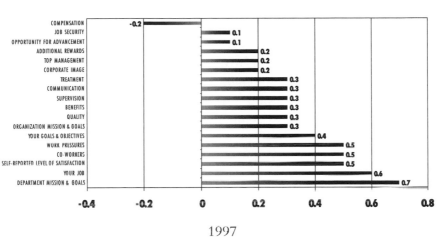

1997

Health Care employees now rate top management at six deviations *above* the norm and consistently respond positively to all eighteen categories of the attitude survey (see Figure 1.2).

FIGURE 1.2d Employee Satisfaction Survey Results.
                (Deviations from Norm)

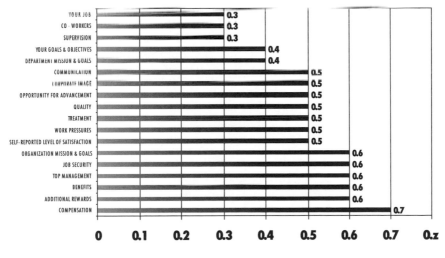

2003

We look forward to getting survey results now—quite a change from those dark days in 1995. Our employees understand that our cultural transformation is real and that we are genuinely committed to their satisfaction. The depth of this transformation was confirmed for all of us when, in 2003, we became only the second healthcare organization to win the Malcolm Baldrige National Quality Award. We would never have received this prestigious honor without a committed and inspired workforce. Every single employee played a part in earning us that award, and in recognition of their contribution, fifty employees from all levels of Baptist Hospital, Inc. went to Washington, D.C. to accompany us as we received the award from President George W. Bush.

The rewards that we experienced from our phenomenal improvement in employee morale are simply too numerous to count. High employee morale leads to service excellence, reduced turnover, and high patient satisfaction. Those, in turn, lead to loyalty and stability, which lead to sustained productivity and profitability. It's a wonderfully rewarding cycle.

THE COMPETITIVE EDGE:
SERVICE EXCELLENCE

I share our story not to boast about how far we have come, but to say that I believe you can do it, too. I am convinced that service excellence can be a competitive advantage for any organization, no matter what service a company provides or what size workforce it supports. When I share the principles that have brought us success with business leaders across the country, they consistently acknowledge that the concepts will apply to their business. More than once, I have been approached by small business owners who confirm my convictions. "I run a five-employee company," one man told me recently, "but we can use the tools you've given us today."

Why am I convinced that an emphasis on service excellence will bring you the success it has brought us? Because quality service creates such a significant advantage against the competition. Through our experience, we have identified several key reasons that unparalleled customer service creates such success. Consider the following four advantages of service excellence:

First, service excellence is created by endowing a workforce with a sense of ownership. This was a foreign concept to us in 1995, and unfortunately remains undiscovered by many healthcare providers in our country today.

Because it is so rare, an organization that is able to create this culture of ownership within its workforce has a high probability of creating a sustainable competitive advantage. The healthcare industry experienced the inverse of this concept in the last decade of the twentieth century when health systems across the country (including ours) began acquiring established, privately owned physician practices. As physicians made the transition from owners to employees, the economic impact—felt nationwide—was disastrous. They taught the entire healthcare industry an expensive lesson about the value of employees maintaining a sense of ownership in their workplace.

The second advantage, which came as an unexpected bonus for us, is that creating a strong, attractive culture results in incredible recruiting power. In a recent nursing orientation session, one of our nurses shared the story of her coming to work at Baptist Hospital. Working as a nurse at another local hospital, she constantly heard stories and comments about the difference at Baptist. Skeptical that any hospital could really be that exceptional, she made a personal, unannounced visit to our campus, not letting anyone know who she was. She walked the halls, talked with families in the waiting room about the care they had received, and questioned employees on duty about their experience working at Baptist Hospital.

After experiencing our culture firsthand, she couldn't argue with the evidence and was soon sitting in our nursing orientation, convinced that the stories she had heard about Baptist Health Care were true.

This nurse's story is not unique. Consider these responses from one recent group of new employees when asked to anonymously finish the statement, "I came to work at Baptist Health Care because . . ."

Of the values, benefits, and reputation of the hospital in the community.

Of the friendly environment and good working staff.

BHC was recommended by a friend who told me they had superior customer and employee service.

I heard that Baptist was a good place to work, and you hear many nice things about them everywhere you go.

I know people that work here and they love it.

Of your reputation of excellence.

All my friends say Baptist has provided the best patient care.

Of the excellent reputation.

Of the standard of excellence, opportunity to add to it, and to reach out to the people and community.

My husband worked for Baptist and I've been waiting for something to open up. I was impressed by the stories he told about the culture.

I was offered another higher paying job at another facility and I chose Baptist because I wanted to enjoy my job.

A great culture attracts great employees, and they become the driving force behind organizational excellence.

The third advantage of service excellence is that it creates loyalty among employees and customers, resulting in less turnover and more word-of-mouth advertising. Naturally, employees who thoroughly enjoy their work will stay with an organization longer than those who are unhappy, and they will also tell others about the satisfaction that they find in their work. Figure 1.3 shows the downward trend that we have experienced in turnover since we began our transformation. Similarly, customers who have experienced superior service at one of our hospitals will gladly tell their friends and family members about their experience, creating new customers for us. Again, this word-of-mouth advertising is more effective than any newspaper or television ad that we could run.

People are most loyal to groups or organizations that help them feel

FIGURE 1.3 Employee Turnover Trend

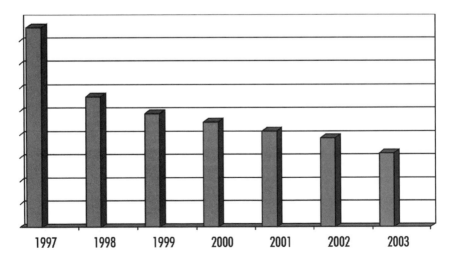

1997   1998   1999   2000   2001   2002   2003

good about themselves. That is one reason that we place so much emphasis on employee satisfaction; we have found that employees who are happy about their work are happier with their lives. And happy people will remain loyal to the things that have made them happy. In turn, satisfied and motivated employees regularly achieve remarkable levels of customer satisfaction, pleasing our customers as well.

A fourth reason to focus your efforts on service excellence is that it affects the organization's immediate and extended family. Service excellence that is achieved through employee satisfaction reaches far beyond our employees to touch every volunteer, physician, patient, and patient's family member. Since we began our transformation eight years ago, our WOW! culture—the acronym means empowering our Workers to become Owners and Winners—also influences our suppliers, partners, patients, and a host of others who come in contact with our organization. Our quest for excellence has become such a basic part of who we are that all who come through our doors are affected by it.

But the advantage doesn't stop there; the benefits of service excellence reach outside the walls of Baptist Health Care. I am convinced that employees who are satisfied, even delighted, with their jobs make better spouses, better parents, better t-ball coaches, better Girl Scout leaders, and the like than those who see their work as a necessary evil. The ripple effect that begins when you create a WOW! culture driven by service excellence has results that are more far-reaching than we can know. Again, this kind of impact can't be easily duplicated by competitors who may enjoy advantages of size, funding, location, or longevity in the market. It is difficult to copy because it is driven, supported, and sustained by the people in the organization.

In your search for the elusive "competitive edge," I encourage you to define the service that you provide and determine how to become the world's best at providing it. When you find ways to maximize the qualities that are unique to your organization while remaining true to your basic guiding principles, you will achieve success. The advantages of creating an environment of service excellence are certainly not limited to the health-care industry. Quality truly can be a powerful competitive advantage in any business, but it will take time, hard work, and unwavering commitment to make it happen. In the rest of this book, I want to outline and define the steps we have taken and the tools we have used to establish a culture where excellence is the standard. It is my hope that you will extract and apply these concepts to your business, turning your own workers into owners and winners—WOW!

FIVE KEYS TO
ACHIEVING SERVICE
AND OPERATIONAL
EXCELLENCE

O ur transformation from a mediocre hospital system to a WOW! organization has enabled us to maintain consistently high levels of service and satisfaction, resulting in local, state, and national recognition. However, I don't believe that the results we have achieved need be limited to our situation. The methods we have used to attain nationally recognized results in the areas of customer and employee satisfaction, turnover, and positive morale, and outstanding quality will work for your organization as well. That is why I have written this book—to share our secrets with you so that you can assimilate and apply them to your business, whatever it is. My aim is to present such compelling evidence of the effectiveness of these techniques that you are convinced that they will work for you. I know they will.

Nothing would please me more than to see organizations across the country begin achieving WOW! results by implementing the ideas from this book. To that end, in 2002 I asked Pam Bilbrey, our Senior Vice President of Corporate Services, to take on a new and exciting role. Having served as leader from day one of our internal corporate training program,

Baptist University, Pam had already demonstrated to me and our entire team that she had both the passion and the talent to take the best practices our employees had created and help other organizations adopt them as their own. I asked her to build a team of consultants from primarily within our culture who could lead other systems to achieve the success we have enjoyed. We have already seen many businesses take advantage of our Baptist Leadership Institute, and I hope to hear of many more companies that have been transformed by internalizing and putting into practice these five keys to achieving service and operational excellence:

Create and Maintain a Great Culture

Select and Retain Great Employees

Commit to Service Excellence

Continuously Develop Great Leaders

Hardwire Success through Systems of Accountability

By focusing our efforts solely on activities prescribed by these five keys, we have made Baptist Health Care a competitive, award-winning organization. Using examples from our own journey and offering practical, how-to guidance for implementation, I hope to demonstrate the power that these five keys have for achieving cultural transformation.

KEY ONE

CREATE AND MAINTAIN A GREAT CULTURE

I n our monthly Baptist Leadership Institute training seminar, which has been attended by over 6,000 healthcare workers from 49 states, wo introduce the first key with this statement:

> Culture will drive strategy
> *or*
> Culture will drag strategy

As I shared earlier, our success hinged on our recognition that lasting change would only come through a complete cultural transformation. When we committed to replacing the negative aspects of our culture with services that would create a WOW! environment, we began to see significant results.

Perhaps the most important question we asked in those early transitional days was, "What do we want our culture to be?" We couldn't succeed in establishing a great culture until we had decided what the end result would look like. In these four chapters, I want to share four foundational elements for creating and maintaining a WOW! culture.

First, you must decide on your overall vision for the organization and commit everything you are to achieving it. I'll outline this process in Chapter 2, Committing to the Mission. Second, you must achieve balance in your quest for excellence. I'll share how we have done this in Chapter 3, Maintaining a Balanced Approach: Pillars of Operational Excellence. Then you must see that your employees become the driving force behind the change. I'll address this in Chapter 4, Fueling Employee-Driven Culture Change. And finally, I want to emphasize in Chapter 5, Engaging Your Workforce: Communicate, Communicate, Communicate! our conviction that you cannot over-communicate to your workforce.

CHAPTER 2

Committing to the Mission

The most effective leader is one who sees and harnesses the transforming power of vision.

—Beth Davis

I don't believe in micromanaging employees. When people have a shared sense of mission, vision, and values, they can effectively work toward common goals and manage themselves and their responsibilities. In effect, this is the true test of culture: Will people live the values and vision even when no one is there to enforce them? Will they voluntarily exhibit behavior consistent with cultural standards? In our case, will they care about the customer or patient, even when they are off duty (and not being paid to care)?

We have found that when employees know and embrace the mission, vision, and values of their organization, they will create the culture you desire. As we examine those three elements more closely, I encourage you to clearly define each of them according to the qualities that make your organization unique. Identifying and consistently living your mission, vision, and values will serve as a powerful motivator toward cultural change.

POWER OF PURPOSE

Our decision to define and rework our mission statement was driven by a desperate need for a common purpose. At the end of the "Merger Mania" phase that consumed us in the early 1990s, we found that we had suddenly doubled our workforce, creating one large corporation out of many previously independent enterprises. While each entity had an understanding of its own purpose, no one had given much thought to our overall mission as an organization. The question, "Who is Baptist Health Care?" was one that we struggled to answer.

Recognizing that unity of purpose would be a crucial factor in establishing our new culture, we gathered senior leaders from every affiliate of our newly expanded organization to become involved in determining who we were as Baptist Health Care. Following an initial two-day brainstorming session, we spent the next four months pondering and discussing the following three questions, which we believed held the answer to the overarching question, "Who are we?":

1. Why do we exist? (What is our mission?)
2. What are we striving to become? (What is our vision?)
3. What guides our everyday behavior? (What are our values?)

Any organization seeking to fully define its purpose must answer all three of these questions. A clear mission statement will provide the foundation for everything that you do; it reminds your customers and employees why your company exists. A vision statement motivates your workers to continually strive for improvement by encouraging them to dream of what they can become. And a clearly identified set of values establishes a framework for acceptable behavior and a standard by which employees can manage and evaluate their own behavior.

WHY DO YOU EXIST?

An effective mission statement taps into the passion of your employees. It reminds them of the reasons they chose their profession in the first place and resonates with the goals and dreams they had when they began their career. When a mission statement expresses the passion of your employees, they will embrace it wholeheartedly.

At the end of our four months of discussion and wordsmithing, we agreed that the following statement captured the mission of our organization:

The mission of Baptist Health Care is to provide superior service based on Christian values to improve the quality of life for people and communities served.

This simple statement identifies the unifying purpose of all Baptist Health Care affiliates. Look with me at each of its four sections:

Provide Superior Service. This reflects our organization-wide emphasis on service excellence. It reminds us to always preserve our customer focus and give the highest priority to providing superior service that customers will recognize and appreciate.

Based on Christian Values. As an organization founded on Baptist principles, we use this clause to tap into the rich values, beliefs, customs, and traditions of Christianity. Any mission statement should either state or reference a set of basic values and beliefs.

To Improve the Quality of Life for the People We Serve. This clause answers the "why?" of our mission. Why do we seek to provide superior service and reflect Christian values? To improve the quality of life for the people we serve—our customers. This statement of purpose is sweeping in its implications. It suggests that our definition of health care goes beyond the doors of our hospitals and clinics, and it reminds our employees that they truly have the power to enrich lives.

To Improve the Quality of Life for the Communities We Serve. The final part of our mission statement has sweeping implications as well. It serves as a reminder that each of our affiliates will either contribute to or detract from the community in which they serve and challenges them to become a vital, contributing member of that community.

At a very basic level, this mission drives us. In everything we do, we stop to ask, "Will this program or initiative fit with our mission? Will it help us provide superior service? Will it reflect Christian values? Will it improve the quality of life for our customers and our community?" If not, then we must choose a different course of action.

I encourage you to take the time to carefully craft your organization's mission statement. It is not just a catchy slogan to use for a year and replace when the next business trend comes along. When your mission statement truly captures the reason that your organization exists, it will become the driving force behind all that you do.

WHAT ARE YOU STRIVING TO BECOME?

Our group of officers and administrators used several tools to guide us through the process of crafting new mission and vision statements for Baptist Health Care. One was Jim Collins and Jerry Porras's business best-seller *Built to Last: Successful Habits of Visionary Companies* (HarperBusiness, 2002). In what has become a business classic, Collins and Porras examine the methods and principles of eighteen world-famous, time-tested companies, all of which "blew away" their competition over a fifty-year period, to identify the common practices that drove their success. We were intrigued and challenged by what the authors found.

One striking characteristic of all eighteen successful organizations was their emphasis on setting "big, hairy, audacious goals," which the authors labeled BHAGs. These companies, from Disney to Wal-Mart to Procter & Gamble, all drive their employees to great accomplishments by encouraging them to dream big dreams. By setting the bar high from the beginning, they have continually achieved impressive results. In some ways, you could say they encourage failure by challenging their workforce to reach beyond what seems possible.

With this in mind, we began to consider the question of our own vision: What were we as a healthcare provider striving to become? What was our BHAG, an ambition so preposterously huge that we could never fully achieve it?

We asked ourselves: Do we want to be the best health system in Pensacola against tough local competition? Remember, at the time we were a long way from reaching even that goal, but we dared to dream bigger. Do we want to be the best health system in our region? In our state? These were also worthy and challenging aims, but we pushed even further.

We wanted to define a vision that would motivate and inspire our workforce to accomplish great things. After considerable discussion and debate, we agreed upon this simple but powerful vision statement:

Our vision is to be the best health system in America.

We believed that this vision would drive us to continually find ways to improve, achieve higher quality, and move to the next level of service excellence in every nook and cranny of Baptist Health Care. In the eight years that have passed since we adopted that vision, we have made great progress toward its achievement, but we couldn't have begun the journey if we had not first imagined it, recorded it, and communicated it. It has served as a powerful motivational tool. It gives everyone, in every part of the organization, something to strive for—their goal is to be the very best.

We expect and encourage all of our employees to search until they find "the best of the best" in their area of expertise and benchmark against them. Our rural hospital administrators find other rural hospital administrators to emulate; our radiology directors locate the best radiology directors in the country and find out how they're doing it; from ER nurses to lab technicians to food service providers, all of our employees are expected to find out who is providing world-class service in their field and learn from them. Our employees know that whatever they do, we want them to be the best at it. That's the beauty of having a powerful vision.

Why set the bar so high? Why do we tell our employees that we will never fully attain our vision? Because, just as athletes raise or lower the level of their play to match their competition, employees will perform to meet the expectations that have been set for them. Everyone aspires to something better. People *want* to be held to a high standard and be the best they can be. So, at Baptist Health Care, we view our lofty vision and the high standards it supports as a healthy discipline. I can tell you this—we would not have achieved half of our success if we had set the bar lower.

As you contemplate a vision statement for your company, I challenge you to think beyond what seems rational. What vision could you place before your employees that would drive them daily to be the best they can be? If you set a lofty goal and then fall just short of reaching it, you will still have much to celebrate, but if you hide behind the security of simple, easily attainable goals, you will never know what amazing things your people could have accomplished. Dare to dream big dreams.

WHAT GUIDES YOUR EVERYDAY BEHAVIOR?

The final component in the question, "Who are you?" addresses your company's core values. What collection of beliefs or principles guides your employees' day-to-day service? Whether they are aware of the values they are expressing or not, your employees reflect a certain set of core beliefs in the service they provide. As we considered this question, we again sought to learn from the eighteen "built to last" organizations in Collins and Porras' book. Interestingly, the authors did not find a universal set of values in all eighteen companies; on the contrary, each organization had a unique set of values based on its own vision and culture. What the authors did find, however, were eighteen companies with value systems that had been clearly defined and effectively disseminated throughout the organization. Every employee knew the values, believed in the values, and lived the values each day.

In our fifty-year history, Baptist Health Care has always had an identified set of values. But as we set out on our journey to excellence, we took a fresh look at them to ensure that they accurately represented the beliefs under which we operate. Defining values as a set of principles that guide our everyday behavior, we agreed upon six core values for our organization:

Integrity: Maintaining the highest standards of behavior. Integrity encompasses honesty, ethics, and doing the right things for the right reasons.

Vision: Looking forward to the future and making decisions necessary to accomplish important goals.

Innovation: Being capable of extraordinary creativity and willing to explore new approaches to improving the quality of life for all persons.

Superior service: Committing to providing excellent service and compassionate care.

Stewardship: Being dedicated to responsible stewardship of Baptist Health Care's assets and financial resources and to community service.

Teamwork: Showing an abiding respect for others and a sustaining commitment to work together.

These six core values support a WOW! culture. Let's examine each of them.

You will not maintain a high-performance culture without *integrity*, starting at the top and cascading down through the organization. We ascribe to the highest standards of professional ethics and etiquette. We believe it matters that we are honest with each other and that we do the right things at the right time for the right reasons.

FIGURE 2.1 Mission, Vision, and Values Statement

Our Mission

*The mission of Baptist Health Care is to provide superior service based on
Christian values to improve the quality of life for people and communities served.*

Our Values

Integrity
Maintaining the highest standards of behavior. Encompasses honesty,
ethics, and doing the right things for the right reasons.

Vision
The ability and willingness to look forward to the future and make
decisions necessary to accomplish important goals.

Innovation
Capable of extraordinary creativity and willing to explore new approaches
to improving quality of life for all persons.

Superior service
Committed to providing excellent service and compassionate care.

Stewardship
Dedicated to responsible stewardship of Baptist Health Care's assets and
financial resources, and to community service.

Teamwork
An abiding respect for others, and a sustaining commitment to work
together.

Our Vision

The vision of Baptist Health Care is to be the best health system in
America.

Vision is essential to maintaining a WOW! culture because it gives people a future to look forward to and a standard for making decisions and taking actions necessary to accomplish important goals. We want every stakeholder in Baptist Health Care looking not at where we are today but at where we can be tomorrow.

Innovation is another "vital organ" in a WOW! culture. In the body of the organization, innovation adds a spirit of exploration and a willingness to try new approaches to improve the quality of life for all constituents. We want to foster an environment that says, "There always has to be a better way to do it—let's find it!"

Superior service is the ultimate goal of the WOW! culture. Exceptional service is, after all, what elicits the WOW! response from customers. To consistently achieve superior service, you have to nourish the spiritual roots from which it springs—commitment and compassion in the hearts of your employees.

Stewardship suggests a deep sense of personal and shared responsibility for the wise use of the assets and resources of the organization. Historically, a steward is a person entrusted with the management of a household or estate of another. In our hospital system, we constantly remind ourselves that we are "owned" by the community and are stewards of one of our community's most precious resources.

Teamwork begins with an abiding respect for others and is sustained through a collective commitment to work well together. It takes a shared understanding of the mission and vision of the organization; myopic views and selfish actions kill teamwork.

After we had developed our mission, vision, and value statements, we had hundreds of copies printed, framed and posted throughout our organization (see Figure 2.1). We have gone to great lengths to ensure that every employee knows our mission, vision, and six core values *and* understands his or her role in helping us to achieve those dreams.

If you haven't already, I encourage you to define your own set of core values and then zealously communicate them to every member of your organization, remembering that the strongest message you send is that of your personal example. When you begin to live out your organization's core values for employees and customers to see, those values will truly become part of your culture.

CHAPTER 3

Maintaining a Balanced Approach: Pillars of Operational Excellence

When the Baldrige examiners said we exhibited a
"maniacal consistency of purpose" with our Five Pillars
of Operational Excellence, I was extremely pleased.
—Al Stubblefield

W hen I am speaking to CEOs across the country, I often ask them two questions: First, what do your employees think that *you* think is really important? And second, how do they know? The answer to the second question, which may seem obvious but escapes far too many business leaders, is this: Your employees know what is important to you by listening to what you talk about—from the interview process and the orientation agenda until the day they leave the organization (hopefully to retire). You may have a heart full of wonderful, culture-changing beliefs and values, but if you never communicate them to your employees, they will not believe that values are important to you. The same truth applies to your board of directors. What issue consumes the majority of time at most hospital board meetings? The runaway answer, without even a close second, is financial concerns. This was certainly the case for us prior to our cultural revolution.

I would venture to say that far too many healthcare employees in America believe that their administrators are concerned only with the bottom line.

Why? Because that is all they hear us talk about! While we must consider profit margins and revenues (we can't stay in business without a profit!), many other issues are just as critical to running a successful corporation. As we began to work through the nuts and bolts of establishing a great culture, we made some important discoveries about the strength of a balanced approach.

As I recounted earlier, we had decided to make **service** excellence our competitive battleground. What I didn't say, but may have implied, was that this was ultimately a **financial** decision for us. We believed that the route to financial stability was to become a "patient magnet" by delivering world-class service. As we sought to improve our service, however, we quickly learned that without bought-in, engaged, committed **people**, our service meter was not going to budge. Finally, we acknowledged that if our clinical **quality** didn't improve, we would never be able to sustain the high levels of patient and employee satisfaction that we desired.

We knew that each of these elements was crucial, but we faced a dilemma: Which emphasis came first? Should we focus on finances first, which would allow for better service, which would enable us to recruit the best people, which would improve our overall quality? Or should we start with service, which would help us get the right people, which would raise the level of quality, which would improve our bottom line? We found that we could argue convincingly to make any one of the four areas our top priority.

As we discussed and debated the best way to focus our initial efforts, it became progressively clearer that we needed to achieve simultaneous success in all four areas—cost, quality, people, and service. In order to attain our vision of becoming the best in the nation, we would have to maintain a consistent and balanced emphasis on each of these critical success factors. Thus, we labeled these categories our *Four Pillars of Operational Excellence*, agreeing to structure all of our efforts as an organization around them. Over the next few years, as we increased our focus on the pillars, we recognized that when we achieved success in those four areas, growth came as a natural result. That discovery led us to add a fifth pillar—the *growth* pillar—to bring the same consistency of focus to expanding and growing every facet of our organization.

As we continued to implement and develop our pillar-focused culture, we made two final changes to the pillars. First, we decided that the term "financial," rather than "cost," would better encompass the whole realm of issues surrounding the use of our monetary resources. We renamed the cost pillar to reflect our core value of stewardship and encourage our employees to think in broader terms about their role in our organization's financial stability. The second change we made grew out of a conviction that the order of the pillars mattered. We determined that people should always come first, because without our employees on board, we could never achieve success in any of the five areas. Service came next, because providing world-class care is key to engaging the hearts of healthcare workers. Quality was third, followed by financial, and finally growth, the natural result of a balanced emphasis on the other four.

These are the Five Pillars of Operational Excellence that you will find throughout our organization to this day:

People

Service

Quality

Financial

Growth

We have spent the last eight years maintaining an unrelenting focus on these areas. They are at the heart of everything we do, and they have permeated our organization and guided our cultural transformation.

We have expressed them in Figure 3.1. This figure is a familiar sight to all of our employees and volunteers, and to many of our customers. We

FIGURE 3.1 Baptist Health Care's Five Pillars of Operational Excellence

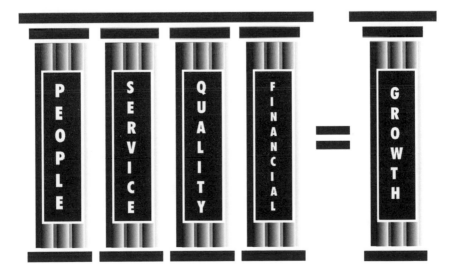

post it in visible locations throughout our campus. We want it to serve as a constant reminder that we are always striving toward improvement in these five areas. As I expressed earlier and as you can see in the figure, we believe that consistent success under the first four pillars will automatically result in growth. These five pillars underpin our commitment to service excellence and to maintaining a WOW! culture.

I admit that I'm basically a numbers guy. I love to look at admissions, revenue, procedures, and percentages of increase and decrease. Before our transformation, that's what I cared about—and it showed, because that's what I talked about. Becoming more balanced in my approach to health-care management has been an important step in my personal transformation, and these pillars are the tool that has made it happen for me.

Thankfully, I haven't had to completely deny my affinity for numbers, charts, and spreadsheets to gain this balanced approach. I can still be a numbers guy, but now I have measures under each pillar. For "people" measurements, I can look at employee turnover, our employee satisfaction survey, or our *Fortune* magazine ranking. I can track numbers for "service" by looking at percentile rankings in all of our measured service categories. Those same kinds of quantifiable measures exist for each pillar, and we continue to find ways to improve in each area.

Our dedication to these five pillars guides everything we do. Every goal that we set as an organization must fall under one of these five areas. Employees are recognized and rewarded for their specific contributions to one of the pillars. The questions on our customer satisfaction surveys address these five specific areas. Employee scripts are developed with the pillars in mind. Every activity that our employees devote time or money to must fall under one of these five headings.

Let me share just a few of the multiple ways that we keep these pillars in front of our employees, customers, and leaders.

ORGANIZATIONAL GOALS

At every level of our organization, employees set goals with these pillars in mind. All of our managers are required to agree with their supervisors on a 90-day action plan for their department, listing goals and activities to be completed under all five pillars.

For example, during one quarter of 2002, our dietary department set goals to reduce turnover (people), maintain a ninety-nine percent patient satisfaction ranking (service), implement three innovative concepts including a café redesign (quality), raise the score on their Budget Accountability Report (financial), and increase retail sales by five percent (growth). Every department has identified ninety-day goals for all five pillars. I will describe our use of ninety-day action plans more fully in Chapter 13, Building a Culture that Holds Employees Accountable.

Each department also sets at least one annual goal for each pillar, using ninety-day action plans to stay on track toward those goals. At the entity level, our leaders at each hospital, nursing home, or other facility establish pillar-based three-year goals for their organization; and finally, we also maintain three-year goals for the entire healthcare system that are clearly aligned with the five pillars. Goals under all five pillars, from system to entity to officer to department level to middle manager—that's alignment.

COMMUNICATION BOARDS

Every department in every entity of Baptist Health Care is required to create and maintain a communication board somewhere in their department. On this board, we ask department managers to keep track of the goals they have set and monitor their department's progress toward those goals. Each communication board is divided into five sections—one for each pillar— and department managers are expected to keep their goals and progress updates current, using the board to both recognize accomplishments and highlight opportunities for improvement.

At our flagship hospital, we also have one large communication wall located outside the cafeteria. In this central, highly visible location, we have actually built five pillars into the wall. Each pillar has its own bulletin board, and we post organization-wide goals on each board as well as recognition of our accomplishments toward reaching those goals. This communication wall, which is visible not only to employees but also to our customers, serves as a constant reminder to focus our efforts around those five pillars (see Figure 3.2).

MEETING AGENDAS

From senior level executives to department heads to individual members of a department, every group of BHC employees that meets together is

FIGURE 3.2 Pillar Wall

expected to structure their meeting around the five pillars. Managers and supervisors use their ninety-day action plans (based on the pillars) to develop meeting agendas like the one in Figure 3.3. In the quarterly employee forums held at each of our hospitals, our administrators make presentations organized around reporting goals and results for each pillar. Even our board meetings are structured in this way, as we systematically look at the pressing issues in all five areas: people, service, quality, financial, and growth.

BAPTIST UNIVERSITY PRESENTATIONS

At each of our quarterly leadership training seminars, attended by 600 Baptist Health Care leaders, I make a pillar-focused presentation. In the weeks leading up to the event, we ask our administrators to report their organization's achievements under each of the five pillars, listing one to three results

FIGURE 3.3 Department Head Meeting Agenda

Department Head
AGENDA
April 21, 2004

OPENING PRAYER

BEST PEOPLE:
  Introductions/Recognitions—John Heer
  Junior Achievement Recognition—Frances Yost
  Champion—Chris York
  Outstanding Leader Award—Phoebe Mayfield
  Turnover
  Late Evaluation Slide

SERVICE:
  Patient Satisfaction
  Standard of the Month April Summary—Janet Day
  Standard of the Month May Roll-out—Maria Pomeroy

QUALITY:
  Pressure Ulcer Trend—Joanie Morse
  Length of stay/CMI—Starla Stavely
  CARE Report

FINANCIAL:
  Productivity—Bill Perkins
  Financial Review—Bill Perkins
  BAR Review—Bill Perkins

GROWTH:
  Growth Results—Bob Murphy
  Construction Update—Earl/Chris
  Market Share

Other:

Baptist Hospital = Main Campus
FY 2004 Goals

BEST PEOPLE — Baptist Health Care should be employer of choice in the market area and a healthcare industry leader in values-based recruitment, employee retention, and leadership
  - Achieve 15.2% employee turnover rate
  - Achieve 60 hours of training and development for all employees

BEST SERVICE — Baptist Health Care must provide compassionate care and service to all customers at a level which continues to set the highest standards in the healthcare industry
  - Achieve a 99th percentile in inpatient, outpatient, ambulatory, home health, LifeFlight, billing, and Behavioral Medicine patient satisfaction survey, and 97th percentile in ER
  - Achieve 82% raw score in physician satisfaction survey

HIGH QUALITY — Baptist Health Care must pursue continuous improvement in the quality and efficiency
  - Achieve C.A.R.E. score of 95
  - Achieve full compliance with HIPAA standards (transaction and code set compliance)

FINANCIAL PERFORMANCE — Baptist Health Care should be the market area's low cost provider, while optimizing
  - Achieve BH main campus operating expense per adjusted admission as a percent of net revenue per adjusted admission of 99%
  - Achieve an operating margin of 1.2%
  - Achieve 2.4 bright ideas per FTE and $2.5 million in cost savings ideas

GROWTH — Baptist Health Care must continue to achieve fiscally responsible growth in service locations, volumes and market share to effectively meet the health care needs of people and communities served.
  - Inpatient admission increase 2%
  - Emergency department visits up 2.4%
  - Outpatient volume (revenue) up 11%

per pillar. At the Baptist University event, after I have made my entrance in the costume of the day (which you'll read more about in Chapter 12, Establishing Ongoing Leadership Training), I read through that list of accomplishments, asking all of the leaders from each entity to stand as we applaud their achievements.

This presentation has two major benefits: First, it holds our administrators accountable for achieving results in all five areas, and second, it demonstrates to all 600 leaders in our organization that I am concerned and excited about each of our affiliates making progress under the five pillars. It is one more way we maintain our focus on the pillars.

ANNUAL MEETING REPORT

Every February we hold our annual meeting, attended by all of our board members and the twenty-seven Corporation members who represent the community as owners of our not-for-profit system. That meeting always includes a presentation of Baptist Health Care's annual goals and achievements, and for the last four years, I have structured that speech around the five pillars. In addition to listing our organizational accomplishments under each pillar, I have also made it a practice to recognize one individual from Baptist Health Care who has achieved something truly remarkable under each pillar. We typically surprise these individuals with this recognition, and it becomes another powerful way to maintain our balanced emphasis.

A PASSION FOR PURPOSE

When we had our first site visit from the Malcolm Baldrige National Quality Award examiners four years ago, they spent three days on our campus, touring our facilities and interviewing over 500 employees. After meeting with several of our board members, one of the examiners commented to me that he had never before seen the "maniacal consistency of purpose" that existed in our organization. "We see it from senior management," he said. "We hear it and see it from the rank and file, and we hear it from your board members."

"Great," I said, "That means it's working." Our unrelentingly passionate focus on these five purposes is what has driven our turnaround and made it possible for us to provide world-class service in a culture that gets people excited—a WOW! culture.

I challenge you to think beyond the bottom line in your business. What are the areas that your people need to know matter to you? How are you showing a commitment to finding and retaining the best people, providing the best service, and maintaining the highest quality as well as improving financial performance? When you establish a consistent, unwavering focus on achievement in all four of these areas, you will have a hard time keeping your business from growing.

In his book *In Search of Excellence* (Warner Books, 1988), excellence guru Tom Peters says that every great company he has ever encountered is run by a "monomaniac with a mission." I suppose I might be considered a monomaniac if by that expression he means one who is singularly focused on what it takes to achieve the mission. What will it take for you to become a monomaniac about achieving balance in your company? Define the areas that need attention and then convince every member of your organization to make those areas the primary focus of all that they do.

Culture change happens most quickly and effectively when your employees decide early to buy into it. We found that we could preach all day about the importance of the five pillars, but unless our frontline workers decided that they would get behind our efforts to change, lasting transformation was almost impossible. In the next chapter, I will address the challenge of "Fueling Employee-Driven Culture Change."

CHAPTER 4

Fueling Employee-Driven Culture Change

*You'll never create and sustain a WOW! environment until
you learn to tap into your greatest resource—your people.*
                                                —Al Stubblefield

N o organization can establish and maintain a healthy culture without an engaged and motivated workforce. The change simply will not last if your people are not behind it. A successful cultural transformation will take place only when every employee decides to sell out to the vision. Keypoint—a culture is only as great as its people decide it will be.

Yet moving your people to the point of decision and beyond that, to action, is no small feat. Convincing employees to raise their sights beyond simply earning a paycheck and become involved in something much greater takes time, determination, and creativity. For most leaders, it takes an adjustment in leadership style and a new approach in relating to employees. While these adjustments can be painful, our leaders will quickly tell you that the rewards far outweigh the sacrifice. Let me share three essentials to placing your culture change firmly in your employees' hands.

1. Start at the top, but don't let it end there. We realized early that you can't fake a commitment to service excellence. Customers and employees alike will see straight through a shallow, half-hearted commitment to culture change. If, however, your employees trust that you are genuinely committed to transforming the culture and to supporting them, they will become willing and eager to take you where you both want to go.

Somewhat ironically, employee-driven culture change must start with senior leadership. It can't end there, or by definition it wouldn't be employee-driven, but without a solid, visible commitment from senior leaders regarding your new culture, your people will never buy into it. When I speak to healthcare leaders across the country, I often use the illustration of a three-legged stool to highlight three keys to effective leadership:

Top management commitment
Real-time measurement and accountability
Ongoing leadership development at every level

I tell these leaders that they must have all three of these "legs" in place in order to maintain stability in their organization. I will address the second and third legs in subsequent chapters, but at this point I want to stress the necessity of top management commitment.

Your senior managers must completely commit to the new culture; they must display a nonnegotiable, no-excuses determination that says, "We are going to do this—no matter what." Anything less will be insufficient to see you through the transformation process. What's more, this commitment must be vocal and visible. It isn't enough for your leaders to believe it; they must communicate and reinforce the message to your employees at every available opportunity. As leaders you will constantly face the temptation to allow other events and activities to distract you; there will always be other fires to put out and other meetings to schedule. But you must recognize that your people are watching. Your employees want to know, "Are you really going to have these employee forums every single quarter? Are you really going to visit our department every day? Are you really going to practice the things you preach?" You must be consistent. Our poor track record with consistency caused many of our employees to take a "this too shall pass" attitude in the early stages of our cultural transformation. Only faithful adherence to the principles we were heralding could convince them that our commitment to change was real and lasting.

Real commitment requires that you remove the obstacles to your vision. You cannot allow your organization's sacred cows, whatever they may be, to hinder your transformation. You also cannot allow a few skeptics to hold your whole company back. As we began to establish our new culture, we found that some of our leaders were simply unable to buy into the new ideals we had committed to. As difficult as it may have been to let them go, we knew that keeping them on would have greatly slowed our transformation. You will have to be tough at times to drive the change you seek, but when you have established and clarified your goals, you can confidently take the steps you need to take to reach them. Remember, one definition of crazy is doing the same thing over and over again and expecting a different result. If you want to experience transformation, you will find that some things have to change. Decide what it will take to establish your new culture, and then move forward with confidence. A wise man once said, "You'll never change what you tolerate."

Pam Bilbrey has shared with me that as she and our Baptist Leadership Institute consultants work with organizations to help them implement the principles in this book, they repeatedly run into the wall of management apathy. Too many leaders say that they want to change their company culture but become hesitant when the change gets too difficult, too personal, or too risky. According to our consultants, you can have all the tools, ideas, principles, and action plans that you need to create a healthy, WOW! culture, but until your employees see that their leaders are serious about making a change, they will not be willing to make changes themselves. It may take some time to convince them that this is not just another passing business trend or "program of the month." Over time, however, by consistently living out the culture that you seek, you will establish a fiercely loyal base of employees who will become the unstoppable force that establishes, supports and sustains a WOW! environment in your workplace.

2. Tap into their passion. Once your leaders have established and begun to demonstrate a solid commitment to culture change, you must give your employees a reason to buy into it as well. Why should they care if the culture changes or not? To show that it does—or should—matter to them, you must tap into the passion that brings your people to work each day. We have found that employees expend much greater effort when we effectively connect with the reasons that they chose health care in the first place. People don't enter the medical profession to achieve a five percent net margin or any other financial goal we may be working toward. They choose health-care to serve and care for others, to improve and save lives, and in doing so to make a difference in the world. What a disconnect can exist between what the caregivers come to work to do every day and what top management expects!

Our job as leaders is to recognize the passion that brings people into our profession and to empower them to live out those dreams. At times we may even have to revive that passion in employees who have allowed the daily frustrations and challenges of their jobs to overshadow their initial motivation. Every employee needs an occasional reminder that their work is about more than a paycheck, that they are making a difference by doing what they do.

Why does passion for the work you do matter? As Richard Chang, author of *The Passion Plan at Work* (Jossey-Bass, 2001), writes:

> Passion fills you with energy and excitement. It gets you up in morning and keeps you awake at night. When you experience it, you lose track of time and become absorbed in the task at hand. It uplifts and inspires you. It heightens your performance and enables you to achieve things you never dreamed possible. Just as we can be inspired by our individual passions, so can organizations be driven and defined by their collective passions. No matter what your business, passion can and should play a vital role. Success is no longer as simple as a solid bottom line. Customers face more options. They expect superior quality and friendly service. Employees find their skills in great demand and require more from the companies that employ them. They expect employers to value them, pay them well, and provide meaning in their work.

That's a tall order. When comedian, author, and motivational speaker Andy Andrews spoke to our leadership team, he echoed the same sentiments: "Your passion is what motivates others to join you in pursuit of your great dream. Passion is a product of the heart. It breeds conviction and turns mediocrity into excellence. With passion you will overcome insurmountable odds and obstacles—you will become unstoppable."

So we never apologize for talking about our passion for health care. Without it, we couldn't have achieved excellence. The most effective way for us to offer superior service was and is to build on the humanitarian reasons that lead people to enter our field in the first place. We do this by shaping our mission and vision statements around those passions, by embracing core values that reflect our passion for health care, and by freeing and empowering our employees to provide the highest level of service possible. We seek to affirm in as many ways as possible that they truly are making a difference. When people believe that their work matters, they find the motivation to do it well.

In that light, my question to you is simple: Why have your people chosen to work in your profession? What motivates them to get out of bed and come to work day after day? Once you know why your employees do what they do, you must shape the culture to fit and fulfill their passion. Since people are your only hope of achieving true and lasting culture change, you must create an environment where they have the freedom and support to do the things they dreamed of doing when they began their career.

3. Encourage maximum participation. The third vital step to securing employee-driven culture change is to fully involve your workers in every aspect of the process. Deciding what you're going to do and telling employees that they have to do it will never bring lasting change. Leaving a few details of your new plans unspecified so that you can have a small amount of employee input won't cut it, either. In order for your people to become the driving force behind your transformation, they must have an active role in the change at every level. They must be the ones to discover and define the new culture. Let me share what this looked like as it happened for us.

We decided that if our goal was to create and maintain a great culture, we first needed to learn what that concept meant to our employees. Over several months, our leaders sat down with numerous employee focus groups and asked for their input. Their response to the question, "What makes a great culture?" became our guide as we sought to make the changes that were necessary to achieve our vision and mission.

COMMUNICATE OPENLY AND OFTEN

As we talked with these employee focus groups about their ideal work culture, four key characteristics seemed to surface again and again. It was clear that—in our employees' minds—these were vital elements to a healthy culture. The first thing our employees told us was that a great culture is built on **open communication.** Prior to 1995, it had been the standard practice of our management team to share only good news with our employees. If we had no good news to share, then they simply didn't hear from us. As a leadership team we felt, somehow, that we were serving our employees well by protecting them from any negative information about their workplace. Before we began our turnaround, our patient satisfaction numbers were sinking lower and lower, but only a few top-level administrators ever saw the results. I suppose we believed that our employees were better off not knowing how bad things were getting.

When we finally asked them, however, our employees told us that in a great culture, leaders communicate consistently and openly with the entire workforce. Not only that, but our employees even said that they should have the opportunity to communicate back to senior management. This was certainly not a regular part of our pretransformation culture.

But they were right. If we expected our employees to take the lead in establishing the new culture, then we needed to listen eagerly to their thoughts and ideas regarding the new environment. Therefore, we made an effort to create an atmosphere of open communication. We went from a culture of "command and control" to one of "ask, listen, and act." We became so intent on communicating regularly and effectively with our employees regarding the new culture that we formed a communications team with the primary task of finding creative ways to continually put the service excellence message in front of our workers. They used tools such as department- and organization-wide communication boards, the Baptist Daily training handout (a one-page document read and discussed by all employees each day), and large meetings such as employee forums and special leadership training events to constantly remind all of us of the change we were working toward. For our cultural transformation to be complete and thorough, our management team had to support and participate in this communication in as many ways as possible.

We also sought to encourage open communication by asking our workers to share their goals, frustrations, dreams, and ideas with us as we embarked on the journey to cultural change. What we found was that once they knew we were serious about wanting their input, our workers became an invaluable source of feedback and suggestions. One way we encouraged this atmosphere of open communication was by asking employees to become involved in the process of setting goals for their department and determining the actions needed to reach them. We also asked for their suggestions for improvement through our Bright Ideas program; this system, which encourages and rewards employees who think critically and creatively to find ways to improve their service, has been one of our greatest morale-boosters while at the same time saving us countless hours and millions of dollars. I will share the details of setting up a Bright Ideas program in Chapter 7, Maximizing Employee Loyalty.

We, as leaders, also began to spend more time outside our offices to provide opportunities for employees to share their impressions of the new culture with us. To this day, the Baptist Hospital administrative team eats lunch as often as possible in the cafeteria, making a point to sit with employees they have not had the chance to meet. Their primary intent is to give staff the opportunity to communicate openly with them. Hospital administrator Bob Murphy hosts a monthly "lunch with Bob" for fifteen randomly selected employees—different employees each month. At this lunch, he asks each worker the same three questions: (1) What do you like most about your job? (2) What can we do better? and (3) What can we do to recognize your boss? Initiating this kind of communication across the organization lets employees know that their opinions matter, and it helps senior leaders to better assess the true condition of the culture.

The practice of senior leader rounding has also encouraged communication between staff and management and emphasized the value of our employees, both of which raise morale and increase retention. Rounding involves spending time daily doing just what it sounds like—making rounds. It requires our leaders to get out of the office and make themselves available to talk with employees, listen to and address their concerns, and recognize exemplary service when they see it.

John Heer, who served as Baptist Hospital President from 2000–2004, was one hundred percent sold on the value of rounding. "It's important to demonstrate to staff that you support their efforts and that their feedback will be used to make the organization better," he said. "Rounding is a great tool to reward and acknowledge your staff's performance or discover areas for improvement. This is your time to engage staff and find out what they need." When he was with us, John was diligent about protecting his "rounding time" each day because he experienced the powerful results that came from spending time with his workforce. In fact, the busier his day was, the more he insisted on rounding. He said that he "didn't have time *not* to round."

Once employees see that their leaders are committed to being available to them, they will become eager to share their experiences. Nurse Leader Bryan Taylor commented, "I've seen employees watching for the leader who's rounding so they can share a personal story or give a suggestion. It's amazing what happens when the team members feel valued and empowered to make changes." Of course, employees must see that their comments are truly making a difference; for instance, if one of our leaders, rounding in a nursing unit, hears a nurse complain about not being able to find blood pressure machines, the leader must do something about it. Ideally, the nurse and the leader should work together to devise a solution, and the leader should follow-up (with e-mail or another visit to the department) to be sure that the situation has improved. You can read more about our rounding practices in Chapter 11, Developing Rounding and Service Recovery Techniques.

What we discovered, when we stopped long enough to listen, was that our employees had remarkable ideas for improving our organization. By creating free-flowing channels of communication that had previously been one-way only, we affirmed that we valued our employees' ideas and insights, and we created a stronger, better organization. It just makes sense that the ones who are on the front lines everyday offering service to our customers will know what they need to do their job most effectively, but too often, managers allow pride or ignorance to keep them from tapping into this vast well of ideas. We had to give up the idea that we knew all the answers and admit that we needed input from our frontline workers. The results have been more beneficial that we can measure.

NO MORE SECRETS

The second thing that our employees consistently told us in the early focus groups was that a great culture has a **"no secrets" environment**. While this idea is closely related to the idea of open communication, our employees felt the need to take that description one step further and call for "no secrets." The employees in those groups shared that they often felt that senior management was hiding things from them. And I will admit that while we eagerly shared the *good* with our workforce, we did our best to keep the *bad* and *ugly* securely contained in the administrative suite.

Of course, in an organization our size, secrets are hard to keep, and our employees did have an idea of what was going on even when we neglected to share it with them. This only reinforced their conviction that they weren't getting the whole story from management. A great culture, each focus group told us, is one where employees know the good, the bad, and the ugly—a "no secrets" environment.

In order to create that sort of environment, our leadership team had to move from "invisible to visible" in as many ways as possible. We did this physically by implementing the senior rounding practices that I mentioned earlier, and we did it figuratively by disseminating and displaying the records and results that we had been keeping to ourselves.

One concrete way that our hospital administrator chose to increase his visibility was by relocating his office to a different area of the facility. Prior to 1996, the administrator of Baptist Hospital worked on the fifth floor of our five-story hospital in an isolated area that contained nothing but a board room and a few offices. The administrative suite had a "penthouse" feel to it, and employees who can remember will tell you that it was a big deal to go to "administration." Staff certainly never just stopped by; in fact, most of them never visited the fifth floor at all.

When I became COO of Baptist Health Care in 1996, I hired Quint Studer to be the Administrator of Baptist Hospital. After six months in the fifth-floor administrative suite, he decided that we needed a change, and relocated to the first floor, in a hallway that leads employees and customers to the cafeteria. Not only was his new office directly on the hallway in a high-traffic area, but he also refused to put any sort of covering on the window to that hallway that stretches the full length of the office. This relocation sent a clear and powerful message to our employees: We have no secrets, and we are available to you. Quint commented that moving his office so dramatically increased his visibility that it actually reduced the amount of time that he needed to spend "out and about." The move boosted morale as well, as our employees no longer perceived management as distant and secretive. We couldn't simply retreat to the penthouse anymore when things got tough. We were now on the level, literally, with our fellow employees.

The second major shift we made in our new "no secrets" culture was in the sharing of our satisfaction scores and financial data. Today, we share results with our employees as soon as we get them. Every Thursday afternoon at 3:00, patient satisfaction scores for the week are e-mailed to everyone in the system. Financial information for Baptist Health Care as a whole is available on the coffee table in administration for anyone who wishes to review it, and specific financials for each department are posted on their communication boards. As I described in Chapter 3, Maintaining a Balanced Approach: Pillars of Operational Excellence, we report our progress and achievements under the five pillars in as many ways as we can. In stark contrast to our pretransformation days, when we get bad news from one of our surveys or reports today, the word spreads more quickly than the good news does. While we always want to take time to enjoy and celebrate our successes, we want our employees to know as quickly as possible when a score has dropped so that we can have "all hands on deck" to bring it back up. How can employees throughout the hospital help a department that is suffering in silence? This public accountability is shocking and a little scary to many healthcare leaders, but when you think of it as a way to hold each other up when we're struggling, it makes sense. That's what a "no secrets" culture is about.

The transparency of having no secrets has proved to be a powerful tool. Employees internalize and take personal responsibility for our success when they see the specific, real-time effects that their work has on our results. For example, if we publish a financial report that shows a negative variance from budget, and the nurses in our Women's Center know that we are running behind our budgeted number of mammograms per day, they are motivated to find ways to raise their volume back to budgeted levels. Because they see all of our financial numbers, they more clearly understand their role in the organization's complete financial picture. A transparent, "no secrets" culture communicates trust and confidence in our employees.

NO MORE EXCUSES

The third characteristic that our original focus groups believed was important in a great culture was a **"no excuses" environment**. Before we began our journey to excellence, instances of making excuses and resistance to change existed unchecked in our organization. The true story of Martha in the mailroom illustrates the dangers of this environment.

After her first few months at Baptist Health Care, a new supervisor was chatting with one of her more seasoned colleagues. The veteran employee asked, "So how do you like it so far at Baptist?"

The new employee was quick to share her pleasure and excitement. "So far I am really liking it. I'm enjoying my work and I'm eager to get to know the system."

"That's great," the veteran responded.

"But there is one thing that is bothering me. I'm afraid that I've offended Martha in the mailroom. For some reason, she has been rude to me ever since I got here."

"Oh, don't worry about her. She treats everyone like that," was the colleague's reply.

And with that, the new supervisor learned the lesson of complacency. In the years before our cultural transformation, employees were quick to make excuses for behaviors that they did not care to change, while we in senior management fostered this atmosphere by regularly explaining away our low satisfaction scores and poor financial results. Changing our culture was going to require all of us to accept personal responsibility for our individual performance and for the success of our organization.

In a "no excuses" environment, employees manage their own morale; in other words, they take responsibility for their attitude and their job performance. There is no substitute for accountability if you want to create a "no excuses" workplace. Workers must know that their job performance will be recorded and evaluated, and that continual poor performance will not be tolerated—no excuses.

In order for this type of environment to be healthy and satisfying to employees, leaders must do two things: (1) they must make performance expectations clear, and (2) they must ensure that employees are fully equipped to do the job that is asked of them. When employees know what is expected of them and have the materials and support to do it well, they will be glad to be held accountable for their performance. They will recognize that a "no excuses" environment pushes them to be their best and become the driving force behind your culture change.

MAKE EVERY EMPLOYEE AN OWNER

Finally, our employees told us that in a great culture, every worker behaves like an **owner**. When Baptist Hospital Administrator Bob Murphy introduces this idea to employees at our Traditions orientation session, he always asks, "How many of you ever put high-quality gas in your cars?" Most employees raise their hands. Then he asks, "How many of you have ever put high-quality gas in a rental car?" The room falls silent every time! Just as the owner of a car or house treats the property differently than a renter would, employees who feel a sense of ownership in their organization behave differently than those who feel they have no stake in their company's success or failure. Owners see their work as a reflection of themselves and take great pride in what they do.

Our employees wanted to feel that they were valued members of a team, not "underlings" who were simply following orders. This was what we wanted, too; we wanted them to feel as valuable as we knew they truly were. Our leadership team was fully aware that unless our employees decided to take the new culture into their own hands, we could never sustain a transformation. With this conviction, we began to take steps to encourage our employees to think like owners.

In Chapter 6, Selecting the Best Employees, you will see that a sense of ownership was one of the characteristics that our employees chose to make a "standard of performance" at Baptist Health Care. This meant that the established, expected behavior was to act like an owner. Therefore, we set out to suggest, encourage, and reward certain owner-like behaviors. For example, we trained employees to remove phrases like "It's not my job" from their vocabulary and instead find the right person to meet a customer's request when they are personally unable to do so. Blaming others for service failures is no longer an option when you take ownership for the organization. Being an owner, we said, means taking personal responsibility for any need that a customer has.

We also decided as an organization that owners take responsibility for the appearance of their workplace; because of this, any employee of Baptist Health Care is responsible for any piece of trash that he sees lying on our campus. This may seem like a small thing, but we have heard comment after comment from visitors to our facilities who are taken aback by our employees' commitment to the appearance of their campus. In fact, when we were named number ten on *Fortune* magazine's "100 Best Places to Work" list in 2001, the editors commented on this simple practice. Who knew that just engaging our employees to clean up would be a cultural differentiator? By assigning this responsibility to every member of our workforce, instead of badmouthing the custodial staff when we see trash in the halls, we demonstrate that we are all on the same team and all expected to do our part. The impact of seeing a senior manager stop to pick up trash on his way down the hall cannot be overstated. When our employees see that we are serious about doing our part, they become owners as well.

Once, when "sense of ownership" was being emphasized as our standard of the month, the Standards team cleverly decided to have t-shirts printed for our Baptist Hospital employees. The front of the shirt read, in bright white letters, "I Own Baptist Hospital." The team encouraged employees to proudly wear their shirts and remember to act like owners at all times.

Not too long after those shirts were given out, we held a dedication service at First Baptist Church as I was installed as the new CEO of Baptist Health Care. As part of that ceremony, an employee choir sang "Amazing

Grace." Standing in the middle of that group, towering over most of his fellow singers at 6 feet, 8 inches tall, was one of our faithful food service workers. All of the Pensacola business leaders who attended that ceremony could read his bright blue t-shirt loudly proclaiming, "I Own Baptist Hospital." I treasure the mental picture I have of that employee, beaming as he sang his heart out, a proud owner of our organization. I believe we sent a powerful message to our community that day about the value we place on every one of our employees.

In a WOW! culture, employees are invited to communicate freely with leaders and enjoy an environment where secrets are not tolerated. A healthy culture also refuses to tolerate excuses for people or their performance. Finally, in a culture that breeds service excellence, every worker thinks and acts like an owner (see Figure 4.1). I believe that if you ask your employees,

FIGURE 4.1 Key Characteristics for a Healthy Culture

as we did, to describe a great culture, they will tell you that these characteristics are just as important in your workplace as they are in ours. There are no shortcuts to creating and maintaining a great culture. You must commit to your organization's mission, vision, and values; achieve balance by identifying your critical service factors and pouring your energy into them; and engage your employees one hundred percent in the process. When you do, you will find that transformation is inevitable.

CHAPTER 5

Engaging Your Workforce: Communicate, Communicate, Communicate!

> *The greatest problem in **communication** is the illusion that it has been accomplished.*
>
> —Daniel W. Davenport

Communication—with employees, with customers, with physicians, with board members, and with the community-at-large—is
at the heart of a WOW! culture. Each of these groups has a critical need to remain "in the know." The more information your employees
have, the better they will understand the elements of your culture, the goals
of the organization, and the value of their contribution. Informed customers
will be more cooperative, more satisfied, and more likely to come back.
Physician involvement is crucial to the success of any healthcare organization,
and effective communication transforms them into partners. Board members
must help set and approve strategies, and they serve as ambassadors for the
organization in the community; they certainly need a clear understanding
of the organization's culture and goals. Public perceptions of the organization
are shaped by information that the community receives from a wide variety of sources. As leaders in a WOW! organization, my senior leaders and I
must be constantly mindful of the need to communicate effectively to all

constituencies. I keep this in mind by frequently invoking a simple mantra: "Communicate, communicate, communicate!"

In our "no secrets" environment, we want our people to have as much useful information as possible. At the same time, we don't want to take valuable time from those who provide our services by asking them to digest complex, lengthy documents. So we strive to communicate information to our employees early and often but keep it as simple and succinct as possible. Effective communication is an art, and it is vital to the establishment of a healthy culture.

Although some of our communication methods are identified and discussed in other chapters of this book, I want to use this chapter to share some of the most important practices we have adopted to make our communication as timely, frequent, and effective as possible.

BHC DAILY

In 2000, we had just begun our quest to win the Baldrige Award and had been awarded a site visit by the Baldrige examiners. On the day that the Baldrige examiners left our campus, I flew with my board chairman to West Palm Beach for a CEO and Board Chairman conference. As we checked into our rooms at the Ritz Carlton, I asked the woman behind the desk, "Didn't your organization just win the Baldrige?" (I knew that they had recently won the award for the second time.)

She began beaming, proudly showed us her Baldrige lapel pin, and even upgraded us to the club floor. (I decided I would try that line every time, but it hasn't worked since!)

We talked with multiple Ritz Carlton employees during our stay, asking about their culture and work environment and confirming that the things we had heard were true. I remembered hearing that the Ritz Carlton conducted ten minutes of training with every employee on every shift, every day. I asked one of the employees I met, "Is it true that you have a regular training time every day?"

"Oh, yes," she said, "I meet with two other employees on this floor every morning. We gather at the coffee pot and go over the 'lineup.' "

"Could I see it?" I asked, and she brought me a copy of that day's sheet, which included statistics about the hotel and a service training point. I was intrigued with the idea.

Two weeks later, Pam Bilbrey was sitting in a Ritz Carlton corporate office with several of their vice presidents on a benchmarking visit. At precisely 9:00 A.M., they all got up and walked into the hall. Ritz Carlton CEO Horst Schulze emerged from his office and shared the "lineup" with his vice presidents. For that day, the service topic they addressed was how to deal with an inebriated hotel guest. Ten minutes later, they were seated in their meeting room again.

When Pam returned from her visit, she shared her story with me, and I related my experience in the hotel. "This is not rocket science," we said, "We can do this." Pam's department got to work developing our own version of the "lineup," and two weeks later the *BHC Daily* was born.

For almost four years now we have been communicating with our employees every day through our *BHC Daily*. Our staff meets in small groups all over Baptist Health Care, at times that are convenient for their department, to share a daily thought and training idea. In our office, we've chosen to meet at 8:45 A.M. every morning, the same time that the Finance Department meets down the hall. Sometimes we wonder why they're laughing louder than we are when we're all supposed to be reading the same information.

The *Daily* is one of the simplest and most effective communication tools we have. Every Friday, Baptist Health Care's Director of People Development e-mails a five-page document containing the *Daily* for the following week to leaders throughout the organization. Each *Daily* is brief (one page), easy to understand, and can be read and discussed in a 5- to 10-minute time frame. Typically, the *Daily* will address different aspects of a single topic each week, with a "wrap-up" on Friday. We select weekly topics that will help drive and sustain our culture, highlighting ideas or practices related to one of our five pillars. We also use it to communicate information about special issues in the organization or community. We occasionally spend a week looking at ways to improve our processes or sharing and discussing financial results (see Figure 5.1).

Many of the department leaders who present the *Daily* to our employees have learned to take full advantage of having all of their staff in one place for a few minutes each day. They use the "lineup" to mention upcoming department activities, acknowledge meaningful events for coworkers (birthdays, employment anniversaries, etc.), and recognize outstanding individual or department achievements. For many of our employees, the "lineup" begins their workday, and department leaders use humor and fun

FIGURE 5.1 BHC Daily Sample

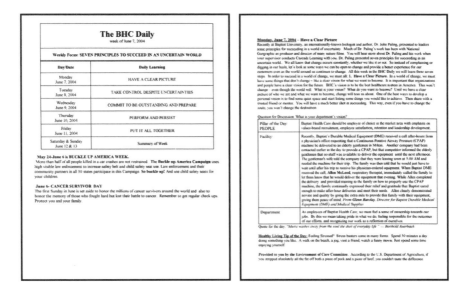

to get their staff off to a positive start. This employee interaction sustains and enhances team spirit and morale and supports our WOW! culture.

The ability to share information and a common message with all Baptist Health Care employees, day in and day out, and to listen and obtain their feedback in discussion, makes the *BHC Daily* a very powerful and highly effective communication tool.

THE INTRANET: INSIDE BAPTIST

Another tool that we use to provide a wealth of information to leaders and employees is our employee intranet, *Inside Baptist.* This electronic system offers employees easy access to information that can help them to stay "in the know" and, ultimately, provide better service to our customers. Through *Inside Baptist,* leaders and employees can obtain key reports on clinical quality, operating data, and financial results. All staff members have constant access to these reports, and leaders especially are held accountable for keeping up with their results.

In addition, employees can access all of our Baptist Health Care policies and procedures through *Inside Baptist,* giving them an easy way to

FIGURE 5.2 Inside Baptist Home Page

refresh themselves on our requirements. Our Bright Ideas program, which I will describe fully in Chapter 7, Maximizing Employee Loyalty, is now handled completely online, as ideas are both submitted and tracked through the intranet. Many forms that our employees use on a daily basis can be accessed and printed through *Inside Baptist.*

Our code of conduct, information on employee benefits, and a discussion forum are available on the Human Resources portion of the site. Also through HR, employees can access a list of job opportunities at Baptist Health Care and print applications. We also keep our staff, board members, and physicians informed and engaged by publishing a series of monthly newsletters: *Doctor's Notes* for physicians; *Management Newsletter* and *The Banner* for employees; *Center Lines* for employees and board members of our behavioral health provider; *Board Briefs* for board members; and *The Standard*, addressing our code of conduct, standards of performance, and ethical behavior in the workplace. While each of these newsletters targets a different group of our constituents, we make the content of each available on *Inside Baptist* for any interested employees to read. We are serious about our "no secrets" culture.

A "News & Events" section of *Inside Baptist* addresses internal and external events affecting the organization, and employees can also reference a daily devotional thought. They can take care of logistical issues like reserving meeting rooms and scanning cafeteria menus and can even purchase clothing with BHC's logo at discounted employee rates. We continuously search for ways to provide more information, more effectively on *Inside Baptist* (see Figure 5.2).

LISTENING AND LEARNING

Communicating information to employees, board members, and physicians is only half of the equation. Listening to their feedback is equally important. Employees are better equipped to do their jobs if they have the information and resources necessary to perform effectively. But they are only truly empowered when we *listen* to what they have to say, whether they have suggestions about better ways to operate or concerns about things that affect our culture and work environment.

As we have built our WOW! culture, we have purposefully tried to create a feedback-rich environment. The more information we have about the perceptions and opinions of our employees, patients, physician partners, and service area residents, the more likely we are to find additional ways to improve our performance and effectiveness, and consequently their levels of satisfaction.

That's why we attach so much importance to our patient, employee, and physician satisfaction surveys and to things like our comparative ranking in *Fortune* magazine's Top 100 Companies to Work for in America. It's why we act on the results we receive, moving rapidly to make improvements when scores for key survey items fall below targets that we have set for ourselves and celebrating when results exceed those same expectations.

We have also implemented a formal *Listening and Learning* program, which more deeply dissects survey results and uses focus groups and market surveys to glean additional information about the needs and perception of our various constituencies. We use the information we obtain to produce a quarterly *Customer Snapshot Report* (see Figure 5.3) highlighting opportunities for improvement for each of our customer groups.

I don't believe we could have achieved and sustained the results we have experienced without developing systematic processes for effectively communicating with and listening to our employees and customers.

FIGURE 5.3 Customer Snapshot Report

Customer Group	Listening & Learning Activities	Opportunities for Improvement	Best Practices	Future Emphasis
Active Patients and Families	Press Ganey Satisfaction Surveys	Comfort of patient rooms and waiting areas; Response to concerns and complaints	Information given to family	Scripting
Potential or Inactive Patients/Community at Large	Women's HeartAdvantage Survey	Many respondents unaware of any hospital heart awareness campaigns; BHC is not the preferred heart care provider	Significant opportunity to influence women at risk for heart disease in areas served by BHC	Focus on education and building awareness
Referring Physicians	Satisfaction survey	Hospital's strategic planning and direction, Physician's rating of their patients' satisfaction with ED services provided	Services provided by Baptist LifeFlight; Depth of Radiologists' reports; Ease of communication with Pharmacy and Radiologists	Communication with physicians
Employees	Reward and Recognition Survey	Not placing emphasis on strategies that are unimportant to employees	Ability to customize Reward and Recognition strategies used for each employee	Make better use of verbal words of thanks given privately
	Administrative/Clerical Employee Focus Groups	Training opportunities in computer skills/BU topics/motivational opportunities	Reward and recognition; Challenging work	Develop training or continuing education program for administrative/clerical staff

TELL THE STORIES

"Those who tell the stories rule the world." A Native American medicine woman said these words, and we have taken them to heart. We know that there is power in telling stories, and we have made a commitment to use the amazing stories that we receive to reinforce our culture and enhance quality.

As I will share in Chapter 8, Celebrating Successes through Reward and Recognition, each month we highlight several stories of employees who have exceeded our customers' expectations in providing excellent care. These employees are identified as *Champions*, and we tell their stories to board members as well as their coworkers. We also use the convenience of e-mail to share the stories we receive more informally with all of our employees. On average, I probably get at least one e-mail per week similar to the one in Figure 5.4.

When we get letters telling about the excellent service that one of our employees provided, we make sure to let that employee and his or her supervisor know that they made a difference. Occasionally, we get a letter that is so powerful we want to share it with everyone. We received one such letter from the friend of a young mother who came to us with a neurological problem and almost died. When we read the letter, we knew we needed to share it with our staff, but we were unsure of the best way to do it. We finally decided to ask the young man to come and read his letter at our upcoming employee forums.

FIGURE 5.4 Sample E-mail

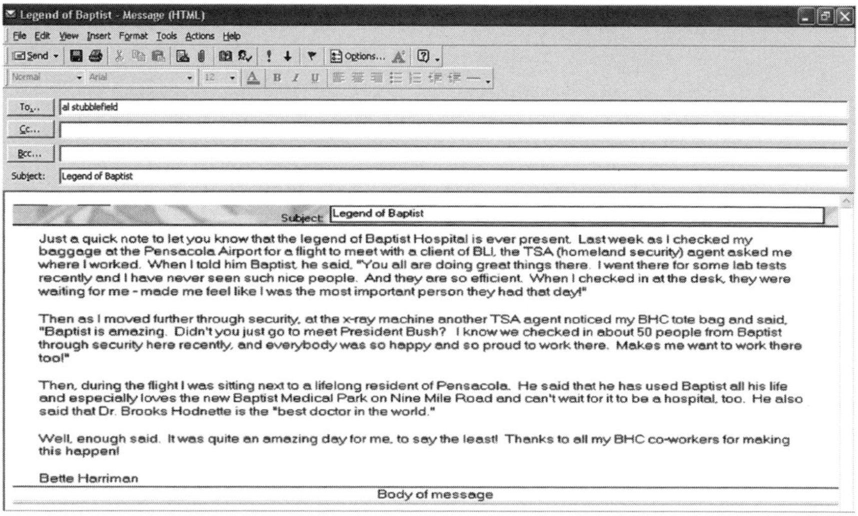

Legend of Baptist - Message (HTML)

To... al stubblefield

Cc...

Bcc...

Subject: Legend of Baptist

Subject: Legend of Baptist

Just a quick note to let you know that the legend of Baptist Hospital is ever present. Last week as I checked my baggage at the Pensacola Airport for a flight to meet with a client of BLI, the TSA (homeland security) agent asked me where I worked. When I told him Baptist, he said, "You all are doing great things there. I went there for some lab tests recently and I have never seen such nice people. And they are so efficient. When I checked in at the desk, they were waiting for me - made me feel like I was the most important person they had that day!"

Then as I moved further through security, at the x-ray machine another TSA agent noticed my BHC tote bag and said, "Baptist is amazing. Didn't you just go to meet President Bush? I know we checked in about 50 people from Baptist through security here recently, and everybody was so happy and so proud to work there. Makes me want to work there too!"

Then, during the flight I was sitting next to a lifelong resident of Pensacola. He said that he has used Baptist all his life and especially loves the new Baptist Medical Park on Nine Mile Road and can't wait for it to be a hospital, too. He also said that Dr. Brooks Hodnette is the "best doctor in the world."

Well, enough said. It was quite an amazing day for me, to say the least! Thanks to all my BHC co-workers for making this happen!

Bette Harriman

Body of message

He initially agreed, but when he learned that we hold seventeen employee forums over a two-week period at various times of the day and night, he wondered if there might be a better way. Someone suggested that we videotape him sharing the letter, and the result has been a powerful tool that we have shown not only to our employees but also to many others who have come to Pensacola to learn from us. The video highlights so many of the things that make our Baptist Health Care culture special, and while it may lose some impact in the translation from the video screen to the printed page, I believe you will see in this transcript why we felt we had to share this story.

VIDEO TRANSCRIPT

(In the video, the bold text appears as a scrolling message while the young man reads the text of the letter.)

> ***Everybody Makes A Difference***
>
> I want to take a moment to thank you and your staff for the excellent treatment given to a very dear and wonderful friend of ours, Michelle.

Everybody Makes a Difference—Emergency Department

Michelle was admitted to your emergency room on Tuesday, October 25. She was quickly diagnosed with a severe subdural bleed in the left side of her brain. Michelle was just six days postpartum and had only been home with her son Corey since the previous Sunday.

Everybody Makes a Difference—Dr. Chapleau

Dr. Chapleau from your neurosurgical staff was forthright, honest, and grave in his assessment of her condition. Due to the size and placement of the bleed, deep within her brain, surgery was held out as a life saving option in an attempt to minimize the possibility of permanent damage. Paralyzed on the right side, unable to speak, Michelle was placed in your Surgical Intensive Nursing Unit and given steroids to manage the situation. While in the SINU Michelle was in the care of several fine professionals who monitored her around the clock.

Everybody Makes a Difference—SINU

While the entire staff deserves mention for their efforts, I am compelled to point out the heroic professionalism of one staff member above all others. A nurse whose name that I know only as Bryan was assigned to Michelle.

Everybody Makes a Difference—Bryan Taylor

While he was kind and caring and understanding at all times, his actions in the early hours of the 27th quite possibly saved the life of a young mother, a cherished friend, and coworker. Brian noticed several small changes in Michelle's vital signs and her neurological assessment. Feeling uncomfortable with these changes, Brian set into motion a CT scan that showed that the bleeding and swelling in the chamber of Michelle's brain had increased. She was only a few hours, possibly minutes away from sure death. Brian's actions gave your surgical staff the opportunity to save a life.

Everybody Makes a Difference—Operating Room Staff

Following surgery Michelle quickly stabilized and was released from the SINU and placed in the neuro step-down ward. While still suffering paralysis and unable to speak, our friend appears to be out of danger. She has been admitted to West Florida's rehab center. On Michelle's last day in Baptist, she uttered her very first words since her injury. "Thank you." It's not much, but it's a start.

Everybody Makes a Difference—Emergency Room Staff, Radiology Staff, SINU Staff

A start that I am sure would never be possible without the upstanding efforts of your emergency room staff, your radiology department, and of course your SINU and surgeons. During our week of anguish and uncertainty her family and friends were treated with compassion and understanding from your entire staff:

Everybody Makes a Difference—Pastoral Care Staff, Dietary Staff, Valet Parking Staff

Waiting room, prayer room, the chapel, the cafeteria. These places became our home as many of us stayed around the clock to be near Michelle. Having these facilities, being able to catch a catnap in a recliner or grab a cup of coffee helped ease our pain and made it possible to concentrate on the prayers that were needed to help Michelle find the strength she needed to fight on. On behalf of all of Michelle's coworkers, her friends, and her family,

All Those That Smiled and Said Hello

I want to thank you and I hope that you will recognize those individuals whose efforts were instrumental in her being alive today. They probably don't know how many lives that Michelle touched or what a bright flame she brings to this world, but I assure you the world is a better place with her in it.

EVERYBODY MAKES A DIFFERENCE

What do you do when you get letters like that? By just sticking them in a file, you are wasting a great resource and a powerful communication tool. As your employees begin to lead the way in developing your own WOW! culture, you are sure to hear some incredible stories. Use them to recognize outstanding service, congratulate deserving employees, and reinforce the emerging culture.

We use many other tools to communicate regularly with our employees. You will read about some of them, like communication boards, employee forums, and cascade learning kits, in other parts of this book. We would be thrilled for you to take some or all of these tools and adapt them to your organization, or you may find that the most effective modes of communication for your company differ from ours. Regardless, I hope that I have sufficiently emphasized that communication is key to driving culture change. You will never engage the hearts of your employees and customers until you make open, frequent, meaningful communication a regular part of your culture.

KEY TWO

SELECT AND RETAIN GREAT EMPLOYEES

I am fond of saying that Baptist Health Care *is* its workforce. We depend on each individual in our organization—from food service workers to nurse leaders to administrators—to sustain and support the culture we have established. In fact, they are the culture! Without staff members who passionately embrace our culture and commit to living it out, we have no hope of lasting change. This conviction has led us to make hiring and retaining the best people a priority from the beginning of our cultural transformation.

In Chapter 6, I will discuss the procedures we use for Selecting the Best Employees, including our use of standards of performance and our practice of peer interviewing. Then, in Chapter 7, Maximizing Employee Loyalty, I will share some of the multiple ways we seek to keep our employees engaged, inspired, and excited about working with us. I have devoted Chapter 8, Celebrating Successes through Reward and Recognition, to describing our practices of reward and recognition—one of the most notable and effective elements of our culture. Employee retention is one of the single most cost-effective measures any organization can develop, and we have gained some valuable insights about this crucial area along our journey.

CHAPTER 6

Selecting the Best Employees

Your most precious possession is not your financial assets. Your most precious possession is the people you have working there, and what they carry around in their heads, and their ability to work together.
—Robert Reich

Hiring the right people is not just a key to improving employee morale—it is essential to long-term success. An employee who has found a job that fits his skills, passion, and personality will work harder, provide better service, and ultimately improve the organization. "At job fairs," says Baptist Health Care Corporate Recruiter Regan Thompson, "we look for enthusiasm for the profession and for our company. Having good credentials is not the only key to being successful." Recognizing the importance of getting the right people on board from the beginning, we have sought to establish a system of hiring employees that will create the highest rates of satisfaction and retention possible. We have found that the process must start early.

STANDARDS OF PERFORMANCE

Our quest to hire and retain the best workers begins before a potential employee ever puts pen to paper. Every person seeking employment at any of our facilities is required to read and agree to comply with our Standards of Performance, which lists specific behaviors that all employees are expected to live out while on duty. Through these standards of performance, potential applicants are made aware of the culture we have established and of the specific expectations we have of our employees. This serves as an early sifting process, since those who cannot comply with the standards our employees have set can simply choose not to apply for a job at Baptist Health Care (see Figure 6.1).

The most powerful aspect of our standards is that they were employee-developed and remain employee-driven. They were developed by our Standards team, which I will discuss in my description of service teams in Chapter 9, Maintaining Quality through Service Teams. Made up of employees from such varied areas as dietary, pharmacy, nursing, and plant operations, the Standards team accepted responsibility for identifying guidelines for employee behavior. We asked them to identify the recurring interactions between our customers and employees and to establish expectations for specific employee behaviors in those situations. Our intent was

FIGURE 6.1 Standard of Performance Agreement on the Application for Employment

TODAY'S DATE:

BAPTIST
HEALTH CARE
An Affiliate of Voluntary Hospitals of America, Inc

HUMAN RESOURCES
910 W. Blount Street, Pensacola, FL 32501 (850) 469-7332
Visit www.ebaptisthealthcare.org

APPLICATION FOR EMPLOYMENT
(TYPE OR PRINT in ink)

It is very important to answer every question completely and honestly. Applications will be active for **60 days** and, after ___ for open posted positions. **Incomplete applications will not be accepted.**

___ n ___ itle(s) you are applying for:

STANDARDS OF PERFORMANCE

A set of performance standards has been developed by the employees of Baptist Health Care to establish specific behaviors that all employees are expected to practice while on duty.

By incorporating these standards as a measure of overall work performance, Baptist Health Care makes it clear that all employees are expected to adhere to and practice the Standards of Performance.

I have read and understand the Standards of Performance, and I agree to comply with and practice the standards outlined within.

___
Signature of Applicant

___
Date

RT 5/04

to outline a set of acceptable behaviors that would become the standard for all of our workers.

The members of the Standards team spent several months benchmarking other organizations and seeking feedback from our customers and employees. They identified key, routine interactions that would occur between customers and employees, including call light responses, telephone conversations, and elevator rides. For each set of circumstances, they outlined a brief but detailed list of standards for employee behavior. When the standards were finally made public, our employees embraced them with surprising eagerness. Because they had played a role in developing and implementing the guidelines, they became their own best motivators toward keeping them.

Our employees identified and specified Standards of Performance for the following ten areas. I have listed just a few of the required behaviors under each category. While this list is not comprehensive, it should help to illustrate the types of actions that have become a regular, expected part of our culture.

Attitude

Promptly welcome your customers in a friendly manner, smiling warmly and introducing yourself. Do not allow anyone to feel ignored.

Meet the customer's need or gladly take him or her to someone who will.

Thank our customers for choosing our hospital.

Appearance

Dress in a manner that is professional, tasteful, tidy, and discreet.

Always wear your identification badge properly.

When you see litter, pick it up and dispose of it properly.

Return all equipment to its proper place.

Communication

Use "please" and "thank you," "sir," and "ma'am" in all conversations when appropriate.

All employees must know how to operate the telephones in their areas. When transferring a call, first provide the caller with the correct number in case the call is disconnected.

Use easily understood and appropriate language when giving patients information about health, special diets, procedures, medications, and so on. Avoid technical or professional jargon.

Never discuss information about patients or hospital business in public areas such as elevators, lobbies, cafeterias, or waiting rooms.

Call Lights

All hospital employees are responsible for answering patients' call lights.

At the nursing station, call lights will be acknowledged by the fifth ring. Address the patient by name and ask, "What can your nurse bring you?"

Check on patients one hour before shift change to minimize patient requests during shift change reports.

Commitment to Coworkers

Treat one another as professionals deserving courtesy, honesty, and respect. Welcome newcomers.

Show consideration. Be sensitive to a fellow employee's inconvenience by avoiding last-minute requests.

Never chastise or embarrass fellow employees in the presence of others.

Customer Waiting

Provide a comfortable atmosphere for waiting customers.

The acceptable waiting time for scheduled appointments is ten minutes; for unscheduled appointments, it is one hour. Apologize if there is a delay, and always thank customers for waiting.

Update family members periodically—at least hourly—while a customer is undergoing a procedure.

Elevator Etiquette

Use the elevator as an opportunity to make a favorable impression. Smile and speak to fellow passengers.

When transporting patients in wheelchairs, always face them toward the door and exit with care. When transporting a patient in a bed or stretcher, politely ask others to wait for another elevator.

If you are escorting someone, hold the elevator door and allow that person to enter first. When leaving the elevator, hold the door if possible.

Privacy

Use discretion in telephone conversations with customers.

Close curtains or doors during examinations, procedures or when otherwise needed.

Provide the proper gown size for customers, and provide a robe or second gown when a patient is walking or in a wheelchair.

Safety Awareness

Report all accidents and incidents promptly and completely.

Protect your back when lifting, pushing, pulling or carrying. Get help when necessary.

Use protective clothing and equipment when appropriate, and be prepared for emergencies.

Sense of Ownership

Keep your work area and surrounding environment clean and safe.

Look beyond your assigned tasks. When it is appropriate for you to perform a service, do so.

Do not say, "It's not my job." If you are unable to meet a request, be responsible for finding someone who can.

Complete tasks. If interrupted, return to the job as soon as possible. If you are unable to finish a task, find someone who can.

BAPTIST BEHAVIORS

Our Standards of Performance are defined and observable, measurable and reportable. Employee Relations Director Teresa Kirkland appreciates the way that the standards set the expectations. "Because they are so clear and easy to interpret, they are valuable when coaching employees who need helpful reminders." Employees know if they are exhibiting a sense of ownership, practicing proper communication methods, or using appropriate elevator etiquette because the guidelines have been set and clearly communicated. There is tremendous peer pressure across our organization to adhere to the standards, and these guidelines have even produced what we call "Baptist Behaviors." These standard-associated behaviors have become commonplace among our employees, but they sometimes take customers or visitors by surprise. For example, I cannot walk across the parking lot or down the hall without picking up trash if I see it. If I do, I violate both the *Appearance* standard and the *Sense of Ownership* standard. Picking up trash—no matter who you are—is a "Baptist Behavior."

One of my favorite "Baptist Behavior," flows out of our *Appearance* standard; we like to call it the "Baptist Shuffle." Most hospitals have tile floors in entrances and hallways. Often the service carts that travel up and down those floors leave scuff marks; however, by applying the hard sole of a shoe to a scuff mark, you can usually erase it. So, if you were to follow me (or any other employee) down the hall at Baptist Hospital, you would be amused to see that every fourth step or so we stop and do a little twist—the Baptist Shuffle. Not only are we enforcing our performance standards related to appearance, but we're also occupying and entertaining ourselves as we walk through the halls. When I'm walking with other employees, we find ourselves racing each other to see who can wipe out the most scuff marks!

Another "Baptist Behavior" that we have adopted is walking people to their destinations. If an employee sees a customer looking lost or confused in one of our facilities, he or she will stop and ask where that customer needs to go. Beyond simply pointing them in the right direction, we ask our employees to walk them all the way to their destination. We make it a point to excuse employees who are late to meetings because they have been escorting our patients or their families. People are often shocked when we show this simple courtesy, which flows directly out of our standards of performance. We have received numerous notes of gratitude in response to this single "Baptist Behavior."

KEEPING THE FOCUS

It was not enough to roll out the standards, get a commitment from employees to follow them, and file those commitments in employee files. These behaviors have become an integral part of our culture because we make a great effort to remind ourselves regularly of our Standards of Performance. One way we continue to reinforce the standards is by highlighting a "standard of the month." We have been emphasizing the same ten standards—one per month—for eight years now, and we have every intention of continuing this practice. Because of this repetition, most of our staff can list all ten standards from memory. Our Standards team finds clever and exciting ways to accentuate each standard. For example, when we were focusing on a *Sense of Ownership* one month, employees were given a button that said, "Owner since ___" and asked to fill in the year that they had come to work at Baptist Hospital. For the rest of that month, every time our employees looked down and saw their buttons, they were reminded to behave like owners.

This team has used crossword puzzles, word searches, employee suggestion boxes, and countless other games and contests to highlight key ideas related to the standard of the month, (see examples in Figure 6.2). Each month they hang banners throughout the hospital to let employees and customers know where we are focusing our attention. They encourage leaders to use department communication boards and the *Baptist Daily* training sheet to address specific ways that their department can live out the standard of the month. And they seek ways to reward and recognize employees who uphold and exceed the performance required by our standards.

By consistently reinforcing all ten Standards of Performance to our employees, we maintain a steady focus on the actions that our employees themselves believe will make us the best. Making these expectations clear from the beginning enables us to hire workers who are committed to upholding the high standards we have set.

FIGURE 6.2 Standard of the Month Puzzles Sample

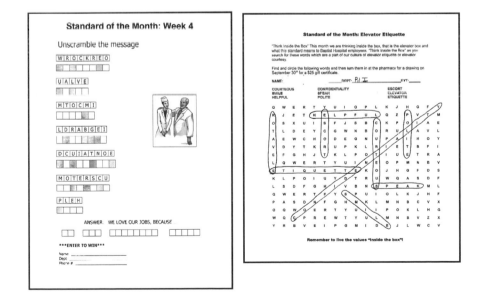

PEER INTERVIEWING

So, we have a candidate who has read and bought in to the standards and says, "I'm the person for this job." We also have a manager who is desperate to get a position filled. Obviously, we make the hire, right? Wrong. At least, not yet.

Another tool that we use to ensure that we are hiring people who fit into our culture is the practice of peer interviewing. Since coworkers play a tremendous role in a new employee's success, we invite them to be actively involved in the selection process. Our reasoning behind this is simple: Who could be a better judge of whether someone will work well on a team than another member of that team?

I directly attribute much of our reduced employee turnover—and the significant financial benefit that comes with it—to the peer interviewing process. Reduced turnover means lowered expenses for recruitment, interviewing, orientation, and training. Our human resources department estimates that the hidden costs incurred in employee replacement can equal as much as two-hundred percent of an employee's base salary; this means that a hospital with 1,000 employees will typically spend over $5 million in employee replacement costs each year. If we can reduce the amount we spend on replacing workers by lowering turnover rates, then we have freed up funds for other areas. We always have more capital requests than we can get to each year. The list of ways we could spend $5 million goes on and on—and I bet your list is just as long.

The benefits of peer interviewing reach far beyond the financial realm, however. Since initiating this practice, we have observed stronger staff support for new hires, promoting a team relationship among coworkers. Our employees can no longer blame their boss for hiring someone who doesn't fit on their team; they are personally responsible, and as a result, we have more cohesive teams across our organization. Peer interviewing also enhances employee satisfaction and engenders a sense of ownership by giving our workers a voice in the selection process. Finally, it improves service by holding coworkers accountable for each other's performance. The sense of responsibility that our workers feel for the success of someone they have helped hire is simply amazing. They will bend over backward to ensure that the new person receives the training and support necessary to do their job well; after all, it is their own judgment that is being evaluated.

Applicants also experience several important benefits through peer interviewing. First, they have the privilege of hearing from those who know the most about the job they want—the ones who are already doing it. They can ask specific questions about job duties and hear honest, straightforward answers from those who are performing similar tasks every day. Applicants can also ask candid questions about the work culture or about leadership that they might hesitate to ask a supervisor or manager. Peer interviewing also gives them an introduction to potential team members and their personalities, allowing applicants to judge for themselves whether the job is a good fit.

Rhonda Yenzer, a nurse in our Cardiac Intensive Care Unit, shared this about her peer interviewing experience: "It was really different to be peer interviewed. In other jobs I had always been hired by the boss. It was great to get an idea of what the job was about and what the people were like. I now peer interview myself. You can feel the way people react. You sense if they'll fit into your team." This development of a "team player" mentality versus the all-too-typical "Who's the new guy?" attitude is one of the most important benefits of peer interviewing.

Not only do our employees get to help select their coworkers through the peer interviewing process, but, when the opportunity arises, they also get to help choose their supervisor. What employee wouldn't jump at the chance to have a role in picking his or her new boss? This is what we allow our staff to do at Baptist Health Care, for the same reasons that we allow them to pick their coworkers. Employees know better than anyone what they need in a leader, and we trust them to look for these qualities as they interview different candidates. When we recently hired a new Manager of Respiratory Therapy at Baptist Hospital, *thirty-two* different people participated in the interview process, including all of our respiratory therapists. Before that manager ever came to work, she had already earned the respect and support of her staff, and they were eager to see her succeed because they had chosen her themselves. That is the power of peer interviewing.

PREPARING FOR THE INTERVIEW

Of course, the peer interviewing process involves much more than just "going with your gut" about a new employee. In order for our employees to determine whether an applicant has the attitude as well as the aptitude to succeed in our culture, they must be armed with appropriate questions as well as the knowledge of what to look for in an applicant. Our employees participate in a two-hour training session in order to become peer interviewers.

As coauthor of the training material, Human Resources Director Celeste Norris designed the curriculum to teach employees how to develop questions to target the right behavior, how to listen in an interview, and how to avoid questions that are inappropriate to ask. We teach our interviewers to ask two main types of questions—skill-based and behavior-based. Skill-based questions enable interviewers to determine whether an applicant has the basic competencies to carry out a job. Before they meet with a potential team member, our interviewers must identify the technical and performance skills the job requires. They ask questions like: Does the job require the use of special machines or equipment? Does it require certain computer abilities? Does it involve managing, supervising, and coaching other employees? Does it involve dealing with other departments or with the public?

Having reviewed the job description and agreed on the skills needed, the team writes out a brief job summary to share with the applicant. Their first task in the interview is to ensure that the applicant is either already capable of doing the job or is willing to acquire the skills that he or she currently lacks. However, these skill-based questions make up only a small part of the entire interview. We encourage teams to spend most of their time asking behavior-based questions that will give insight into a candidate's values, attitude, and work ethic (see Figure 6.3).

We ask behavior-based questions to find out how candidates performed in their previous jobs, believing that past behavior is a fairly reliable indicator of future performance. We encourage our interviewers to listen for specific behaviors that either will or will not fit the culture we have established. Our peer interviewers ask behavior-based questions based on the specific job they are seeking to fill; some of these topics may include goal setting, communication skills, flexibility, supervision, problem solving, planning, organizing, and creativity. What makes these questions behavior-based is that they ask not for a candidate's opinions or beliefs about a topic but for concrete examples of how they have demonstrated those convictions.

For example, in a recent interview with an administrative candidate whose job requires the facilitation of board retreats, the interviewing team asked, "Please list the steps you would take to plan a board retreat. When you last coordinated a management retreat, what were some of the lessons you learned in ensuring a successful experience?" To learn about an applicant's practice of goal setting, a team might ask, "What is an important goal that you've set in the past, and what did you accomplish because of it?" Or

FIGURE 6.3 Interviewing Questions Sample

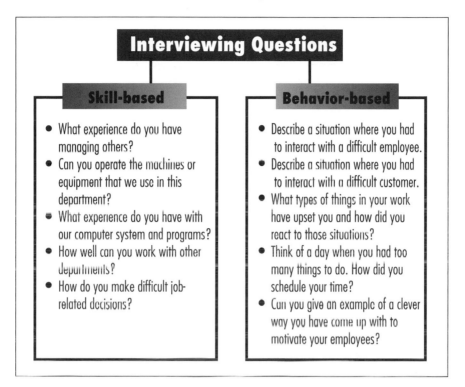

Interviewing Questions

Skill-based

- What experience do you have managing others?
- Can you operate the machines or equipment that we use in this department?
- What experience do you have with our computer system and programs?
- How well can you work with other departments?
- How do you make difficult job-related decisions?

Behavior-based

- Describe a situation where you had to interact with a difficult employee.
- Describe a situation where you had to interact with a difficult customer.
- What types of things in your work have upset you and how did you react to those situations?
- Think of a day when you had too many things to do. How did you schedule your time?
- Can you give an example of a clever way you have come up with to motivate your employees?

to evaluate flexibility: "What methods or processes have you used when you were facing a transitional change in your job responsibilities to ensure a positive outcome for you and the company?" Instead of just saying, "Yes, I think goal setting is important," or, "Yes, I can be flexible," the applicant must now provide a specific example of a time when he has set goals and demonstrated flexibility. While the system is not fool-proof, we have found that the vast majority of the time, our employees know whether someone is a good fit for their team.

There have been times when members of management have recommended someone for a position only to have the team of interviewers tell us, "We don't think he would fit here," or "She doesn't have the right values." I admit that at first it was difficult to let go and trust our employees with those hiring decisions, but they have consistently proven themselves worthy of our trust. Our employees recognize that we are counting on them to help us hire the very best employees, and they take their jobs as peer interviewers very seriously.

I encourage you to use your most valuable resource—your employees—to increase your ability to select the best workers. You can find more detailed information in *Peer Interviewing* (Baptist Leadership Institute, 2004), a book in our Baptist Health Care Best Practices Series.

CHAPTER 7

Maximizing Employee Loyalty

When you're part of a team, you stand up for your teammates. Your loyalty is to them. You protect them through good and bad, because they'd do the same for you.

—Yogi Berra

Our goal at Baptist Health Care is to maintain our position as an employer of choice in our market area, and we know that this will only happen if we remain committed to supporting, training, developing, and rewarding our people. We can't hope to fulfill our vision of being the best healthcare provider in the nation without hiring—and *retaining*—an excellent workforce. Until every employee is sold on and engaged in what we are trying to do, we will never be able to deliver consistent world-class service to our customers.

By the time new employees are hired to work at Baptist Health Care, they have agreed to live by our Standards of Performance and undergone a thorough interview with a group of peers; at this point they should have a clear understanding of our culture and expectations. However, we don't just turn them loose with the mission to "Go provide great service." We have initiated numerous programs and practices to keep our employees educated, motivated, and inspired.

SEE THAT THEY START OUT STRONG

A unique and powerful tool that we utilize in our quest to educate and inspire our people is our *Traditions* two-day hospital orientation. When we use these two days—which are required for all new employees—to introduce, explain, and promote the culture that has driven our transformation, we increase the chances that our new staff will succeed. By clarifying our expectations from the beginning, we allow employees to begin meeting and exceeding those requirements from their first day on the job. Several elements of our Traditions sessions make it the unique and effective tool that it is. Let me share some of the innovative things we do.

Today's Traditions sessions stand in stark contrast to the hospital orientation I attended when I joined the Baptist Hospital team in 1985. Baptist Hospital Administrator Bob Murphy recalls that he brought a book to read during his orientation session, because "half of it didn't apply to me, and the other half I didn't care about." He is not alone in his sentiment; health-care workers across the country dread the dry, stale orientation that is the industry norm. Today, Bob plays a major role in Traditions, and he will passionately testify to the value it has.

One of the greatest aspects of our orientation is the amount of time we devote to culture orientation activities—about eight out of the sixteen hours. While a typical hospital administrator may spend ten to twenty minutes in orientation, our administrator presents the first *two hours* of Traditions, all of which deals with our culture. As a result, culture is the very first thing our new employees hear us talking about. When people join our organization, they have often worked in at least one other healthcare organization. It would be easy for them to think, "Hey, all hospitals are the same. I'll do the same things and behave in the same way I did at my previous employer." We need to prepare our new employees to adjust their expectations—of themselves, of the service they will provide, and of the supervision they will receive. There is a good chance that the service they provided at the other hospital won't cut it here. They need to know that they are about to be held more accountable than they ever have been before. But they also need to know they will be developed more than ever before.

The administrator begins by asking employees to stand and join him in the "Baptist Cheer," yelling, "Gimme a B! Gimme an A!" and so on. Later, when we ask employees what they thought about doing this, they share comments like, "I knew this place was different" and "I thought it was inspiring." This enthusiastic introduction to working at Baptist Hospital clearly makes an impression on new employees.

We've had lots of laughs using our "Baptist Cheer" through the years. In March 2004, we took a group of employees with us to accept the Baldrige National Quality Award from President George W. Bush. After we accepted our award, we led the cheer from the stage, and our employees eagerly participated from the audience. When we had finished, President Bush commented that he wasn't sure if we were Baptist or Pentecostal!

Following the cheer at Traditions, the new employees participate in an exercise that helps them to identify our five pillars. The administrator shows a slide of four intertwining circles (see Figure 7.1) and tells the group, "You have been promoted and you are now the hospital president. In your new job, where are you going to focus? As president, what areas will you give attention to?" He then leaves the room and allows them to brainstorm for a few minutes. Without fail, the new employees identify four areas: people, service, quality, and financial performance. While they may not use identical terminology, they consistently focus on these four areas. In doing so, these brand new employees demonstrate the importance of our first four

FIGURE 7.1 Traditions Opening Activity

pillars. The administrator then goes on to explain how those four areas connect to lead to growth for the organization—our fifth and final pillar.

Why is this activity so valuable? Because within one hour of arriving at their new workplace, our employees have already reached alignment with the five factors around which our culture is built. They have seen this focus from the administrator, and they themselves have identified the importance of each area. They have taught themselves one of the keys to our culture in their first day on the job, rather than learning it slowly over six months or more. The sooner they learn these lessons, the sooner they can start living them out.

The administrator leads our new staff through one more important culture exercise in those first two hours. He asks them to make two lists: (1) characteristics of a great culture and (2) characteristics of a great leader. They then discuss the lists they have compiled, recognizing the ways they can contribute to establishing the culture they desire. Following each Traditions sessions, our Human Resources (HR) department sends the lists to every department head in our organization with a note like this:

> On April 12th & 13th the Baptist Traditions class created lists of the characteristics they found most desirable in a Great Leader and Work Culture. Please take some time to review the attached lists and ensure that we are meeting their expectations. If you see any areas that are lacking, please submit a Bright Idea or attend a leadership development class! (See Figure 7.2.)

I look forward to getting that e-mail and seeing the expectations that our newest group of employees has. It is a wonderful reminder to me and to all of our leaders that we can never stop striving to create a great culture.

While much of the Traditions time is spent meeting regulatory requirements for orientation—it wouldn't be orientation if we didn't cover payroll, benefits, and risk management—we also seek to incorporate as many fun and engaging activities as possible, including a treasure hunt to help employees learn the facility and a motivational message from one of our administrators. And we end the two days the same way we began—talking about culture. Hospital Administrator Bob Murphy devotes the last hour of Traditions to a discussion of "service excellence," teaching employees some of our most common scripts, emphasizing ownership behaviors, and overviewing our service recovery procedures. Before they have completed their second day on the job, Bob has taught employees that we pick up trash everywhere we go, we do the "Baptist Shuffle" when we walk the halls, and

FIGURE 7.2 Characteristics of a Great Leader and Work Culture Sample

Characteristics of a Great Leader

▪ Listening	▪ Integrity	▪ Change facilitator
▪ Visionary	▪ Intelligent	▪ Patient
▪ Responsible	▪ Flexible	▪ Enthusiastic
▪ Open minded	▪ Disciplined	▪ Compassionate
▪ Diplomatic	▪ Enforces standards	▪ Skilled
▪ Encouraging	▪ Handle pressure	▪ Diligent
▪ Good follow-up	▪ Accept feedback	▪ Communication
▪ Consistent	▪ Understands organization	▪ Recognition
▪ Honest	▪ Approachable	▪ Compromise

Characteristics of a Great Work Culture

▪ Open minded	▪ Friendly	▪ Well supplied
▪ Enjoy environment	▪ Safe	▪ Open to change
▪ Work ethic	▪ Supportive	▪ Stable
▪ Holistic approach	▪ Convenient	▪ Caring concern
▪ Team	▪ Rewarding	▪ Diversity
▪ Open communication	▪ Encouraging	▪ Responsible for good
▪ Honesty	▪ Organized	leadership
▪ Hygiene		

we take visitors all the way to their destinations. From this point on, they are all accountable for these "Baptist Behaviors"; we don't have to wait and hope they pick them up somewhere in their first few months on the job. They already know exactly what we expect of them.

I cannot overemphasize the value of this early accountability and alignment. We view our Traditions sessions as a powerful retention tool because they do so much to inspire, educate, and motivate our new employees. When they enter their new jobs with a clear understanding of our expectations and of their roles, they are less likely to experience the disillusionment or disappointment that leads to high initial turnover. We gladly invest our time and resources into culture orientation because we believe we will reap the benefits of engaged, bought-in employees.

OUR SHINING STAR

In 1985 we opened a sixty-bed satellite hospital facility in the affluent suburban community of Gulf Breeze. Dick Fulford, who has been the administrator there from day one, knew as he assembled his team that they faced a significant challenge. Gulf Breeze residents were accustomed to driving across the Pensacola Bay Bridge into Pensacola to satisfy most of their economic as well as healthcare needs. In order to succeed, the new hospital team would have to change those longstanding habits.

He challenged his team to create a level of service that would WOW! the residents of Gulf Breeze, and they did just that. He recognized that the first step toward achieving and maintaining this exceptional status would be a first-class team of managers and staff. They instituted the following "Principles of Management" for the recruitment of the charter leadership team and still live by them today:

> Outstanding results are achieved through teamwork by highly motivated and capable people working together for excellence.

> People are motivated to perform in a superior manner when they are treated with fairness, respect, and dignity, and allowed to participate in decisions affecting them.

> Devoting time to the needs and problems of people, communicating freely with them, and achieving teamwork are the foundations upon which we want to build our organization.

These principles and their enforcement are the foundation on which the Gulf Breeze Hospital team was built and is sustained.

The orientation process for new staff members has remained consistent and includes a welcoming presentation by Dick, who personally reiterates the commitment of the Gulf Breeze Hospital workforce to the community it serves. From the beginning, he sets the expectation of personalized, professional care from all employees. Staff members learn to make it their top priority to handle the smallest of details where the customer is concerned.

In orientation, leaders foster a relaxed atmosphere, encouraging open exchange between new employees and the various speakers.

At orientation, all staff members make three major pledges that empower them to reach across traditional workplace boundaries. First, they pledge to never use the statement, "It's not my job." Second, all members commit to reducing or eliminating hassles for the customer. The third pledge is to provide personalized, professional care at all times.

In the orientation session, Dick emphasizes that every person working at Gulf Breeze Hospital has the opportunity to make a customer's interaction exceptional by being perceptive to inconveniences and eliminating them regardless of whether it is stated in their job description or not. In fact, employees not only have this opportunity, but they have committed to this level of customer focus before completing the interviewing and hiring process. Dick concludes with a familiar theme—that the culture at Gulf Breeze Hospital encourages teamwork, commitment to coworkers, open communication, and a positive "can do" attitude.

When Baptist Health Care started its cultural transformation, what we didn't realize was that in many ways Gulf Breeze was already way ahead of us. In 1996 I asked Dick to begin using the *Press, Ganey* patient satisfaction instrument so that he could compare his hospital to others in an external database. I explained that my request came from our belief that measurement and benchmarking are vital to improvement. I remember that Dick was reluctant to change because he was satisfied with the survey that Gulf Breeze was using. As a good team player, he agreed to switch and was glad that he did when they received their first feedback report and learned that they were the number one hospital in the country in patient satisfaction. Amazingly, Gulf Breeze has maintained that position for 100 consecutive months. WOW! They quickly became our internal benchmark organization as we sought to duplicate across our system the cultural and service quality that have produced their incredible results.

KEEP THEM ENGAGED

While we believe that the things we teach at orientation sessions are valuable and meaningful for our employees, we also understand that they are not going to remember everything that they hear in those sixteen hours without an occasional review. That conviction, coupled with the knowledge that most organizations experience the highest turnover with staff members who have been employed less than six months, led us to create

ServU, a half-day refresher course covering the most important culture elements from Traditions. We invite employees who have been with us for more than ninety days but less than six months to attend ServU, which is offered every other month. By taking employees off the job for a day after they have been working for a few months, they are able to make better application than they can in new hire orientation.

The day actually begins with a review of Traditions led by Bob Murphy, the same leader who closes the orientation sessions. Bob intentionally begins by linking employees back to the things they learned at Traditions, reminding them of our quest for service excellence and our emphasis on the people in our organization. Other topics at ServU include Measurement 101—how and why we measure customer satisfaction; Bright Ideas, which I will discuss later in this chapter; Standards of Performance—a review of the behaviors we expect from our staff; and Loyalty Teams—a description of each of our five teams and an invitation to serve on a team. Each ServU session yields several new volunteers to serve on our loyalty teams.

The most popular element of ServU is a demonstration of scripting by a lab team from the hospital. They present a "before and after" skit showing the dangers of poor scripting and the value of proper scripting. Employees love this lighthearted look at one of our best practices, and while they are laughing, they are also learning to do their job more effectively. The day ends with a brief graduation ceremony and group photo, and then we send them back to their departments to practice what they have learned.

Asking our employees to spend a day focusing on the things that have brought us success brings us into closer alignment as an organizational family, and it keeps our employees' hearts and minds engaged in what we are trying to do. We became so convinced of the value of ServU that we even began inviting seasoned employees to attend a session. Some of our ServU graduates have been working at Baptist for over thirty years! Everyone can use an occasional reminder of the most important aspects of their job. ServU keeps us all on the same page, and it keeps employees excited about being a member of the Baptist Health Care team.

EMPLOYEE FORUMS

Another way that we seek to keep our employees connected is through quarterly employee forums at each Baptist Health Care entity. These town-hall-style, one-hour sessions are offered multiple times each quarter to ensure that all employees will have a chance to attend. For example, at Baptist Hospital we hold seventeen employee forums over a two-week period. We offer one forum at midnight on Friday night, one on Saturday afternoon, and others during early morning hours to accommodate employees who work off-hours. Attendance at forums is not mandatory, but is very strongly encouraged; leaders are accountable for their staff's attendance.

Our leaders use employee forums to communicate goals, celebrate results, discuss upcoming special events, and address special topics of concern. One of the main purposes of the forums is to give administrators a chance to speak directly to their staff. We want to avoid the problem illustrated by the childhood game "Telephone," where a message is distorted as it is whispered from one person to another. In our case, we want the message to travel straight from an administrator's mouth to an employee's ears, leaving little chance for alteration. We also leave time at the end of each forum for questions and dialog, encouraging employees to clarify misunderstandings and voice their concerns and ideas.

We so highly value the two-way communication that takes place at employee forums that we encourage attendance in a number of ways. First, we try to make it as fun as possible. Choosing a different theme each quarter, a leadership team prepares t-shirts for management and incorporates games and door prizes. For example, last year in preparation for our Joint Commission Survey, employees at each forum played a round of Joint Commission Jeopardy. At another forum, Bob Murphy transformed into cartoon character Bob the Builder to present the information. During the "Who Wants to Be a Millionaire?" craze, our employees played our own version of "Who Wants to Be a Baptist aire?"

We also encourage attendance by offering *continuing education units* (CEUs) for forum attendance. Nurses and other staff must accumulate a certain number of units each year, and providing them for attending forums makes that hour even more valuable for these employees. Recognizing that their time is precious, we also reward employees for their attendance; at Baptist Hospital, employees receive an "I Attended" button (pictured in Figure 7.3) that can be redeemed for an ice cream cone in the cafeteria. The button serves double-duty, both as a reward for those who attended and as an advertising reminder for those who still need to attend a forum.

Employee forums serve as a valuable tool in maintaining open communication between our leaders and employees, and they keep the most important

FIGURE 7.3 "I Attended" Button from Employee Forums

aspects of our culture elevated to a place of significance. They are another crucial element in our effort to keep employees engaged and educated.

USE THEIR BRIGHT IDEAS

Ken Derr, chairman and CEO of Chevron, has said, "Every day that a better idea goes unused is a lost opportunity. We have to share more, and we have to share faster." This conviction sums up the motivation behind our Bright Ideas program, which has been another key factor in engaging and retaining our workforce.

We realized early in our journey to excellence that in order to achieve success, every employee must believe that he or she is important to the organization. Employees who feel valued become inspired, motivated workers. We also realized that employee creativity and resourcefulness is a powerful, yet often overlooked, tool for achieving excellence. When we decided to begin asking our workers for their insights concerning the changes needed in their area of specialty instead of just relying on our own impressions, our *Bright Ideas* program was born.

At Baptist Health Care, a Bright Idea is any suggestion on how we can better serve our patients, employees, or community. It leads to a positive change in our organization and saves time or money—or both. It must also fall under one of our Five Pillars of Operational Excellence and be within the capacity of our resources to be implemented as a Bright Idea.

Here are just a few of the ideas we have implemented over the last several years:

People Pillar

Idea: Have phlebotomists do patient rounds every day to identify patient problems and complaints.

Benefit: Correct problems, interact with patients, improve patient satisfaction.

Department: Lab Outreach

Service Pillar

Idea: Provide free flu vaccine to community service organizations including the Health Department and Community Clinic. We had not-returnable flu vaccine left over that would go to waste if not used.

Benefit: Utilize excess flu vaccine for indigent care.

Department: BHC Towers Pharmacy

Quality Pillar

Idea: When a patient is discharged and has a follow-up doctor's appointment, fax the face sheet, psychosocial and lab reports and discharge summary to the doctor's office on the discharge day.

Benefit: The physician has current information about the patient's treatment during the hospital stay. This expedites patient care and creates physician satisfaction.

Department: Behavioral Medicine

Financial Pillar

Idea: Set up Cardiac Cath trays for intervention only when the physician indicates, not on every case.

Benefit: This saves the expense of the heparinized saline bag, the bag decanter, the bottle of Hypaque, 2-20cc syringes, 2 needles, one 12cc syringe and 3-30cc syringes and extra towels for each case.

Annual Financial Impact: $48,000

Department: Cardiac Cath Lab

Growth Pillar

Idea: Create a "menu" of sorts for physicians performing gastric bypass surgery, detailing pre- and post-op procedures required or recommended. Also include an at-a-glance payer criteria for reimbursement.

Benefit: Improved pre- and post-operative procedures and timeliness of scheduling, increased referrals for outpatient procedures, ease of ordering for doctors.

Department: Financial Planning

In the year 2000, our Bright Ideas program was still in its early stages. We were averaging less than one *submitted* idea per full-time employee each year and were only *implementing* about one in six of those submitted ideas. Determined to make better use of our employees' creativity and ingenuity, I challenged our leaders to raise their sights for the next year, setting a goal of at least one *implemented* Bright Idea per full-time employee. This was a big jump to take, and my leadership team offered plenty of arguments against it: "We can't get employees to submit that many good ideas. Plus, we don't have the systems in place to implement them. What if we just aim for one *submitted* idea per full-time employee?"

Undaunted, I asked the leadership team, "Are you telling me that in 365 days we can't implement one Bright Idea per full-time employee?" I was convinced that this was not too much to ask, and so our team of leaders stood behind me as we decided to press on toward that goal.

As they have throughout this transformation process, our employees rose to the challenge we presented them, surpassing our 2001 goal with an average of 1.2 implemented ideas per full-time employee; we estimate that the 4,000-plus ideas that we implemented that year saved us $2.5 million. Our goal for 2001 was 1.5, and we implemented 1.8 ideas per employee for

$2.9 million in cost savings. We have raised and surpassed our goals for implemented Bright Ideas every year since 2000, and we estimate that since the program's inception, we have implemented over 25,000 ideas that have brought over $20 million in cost savings and revenue enhancements. We have unleashed the power of our employees' minds—a strength that we never knew we had until we found a way to capture these ideas.

As wonderful as those savings are, they are not the greatest benefit of a Bright Ideas program. Recently, I stepped into an elevator with an employee that I hadn't seen in a while. Thinking she might have retired, I told her, "I've missed seeing you around here."

"Oh, I've transferred to Lakeview," she told me. Lakeview Center is our behavioral medicine facility.

"Are you enjoying it there?" I asked.

"Yes," she said, and her face lit up as she announced, "They just implemented two of my Bright Ideas."

That encounter reinforced to me the power of making sure our employees know that we want and need them for more than just their bodies and licenses—we want their minds, their ideas, and their total participation in our organization. A program like Bright Ideas reminds employees that we value their expertise and wisdom, and it encourages the sense of ownership that is vital to long-term success. I strongly encourage you to consider using a similar program in your organization. One of our most sought-after materials is the *Bright Ideas* (Baptist Health Care Leadership Institute, 2004) book from the Baptist Health Care Best Practices Series (see Figure 7.4). It outlines the nuts and bolts of establishing a successful Bright Ideas program. At the request of colleagues across the country, we also now make available the software that we developed internally to manage the Bright Ideas program.

BRIGHT IDEA PROCESS

Let me briefly describe the process that we have developed for submitting, implementing, and rewarding Bright Ideas.

The first step to Bright Idea submission is for leaders and supervisors to promote the program and encourage employee participation. They do this by clearly explaining the submission process, recognizing and rewarding participation, stressing the value that Bright Ideas add to our organization, and by making it fun for members of their department to participate. Our

FIGURE 7.4 *Bright Ideas* Book from Best Practices Series

BAPTIST HEALTH CARE BEST PRACTICES SERIES

brightideas

BAPTIST HEALTH CARE
Leadership Institute

attitude concerning Bright Idea submission is "the more the merrier." Often, in the process of sorting through several suggestions, leaders will discover that the best solution is a combination of one or more ideas. We never want to miss out on the best ideas by limiting our expectations and settling for only one or two suggestions.

When an employee formulates an idea to submit, he or she can use our online submission form or submit a paper copy of the form to a department leader. The leader then reviews the idea and either submits it to our Bright Ideas system or works with the employee to rework the idea into an implementable concept. Once it is ready for submission, the idea travels to the Bright Ideas coordinator, who officially enters it into the system and assigns it to the appropriate department leader.

That leader then reviews the idea and chooses one of four courses of action: (1) accept responsibility for the idea and set a target date for implementation; (2) reject responsibility and forward it to another person or department; (3) close the idea, stating why it is not feasible; or (4) implement the idea immediately. Supervisors have thirty days to take one of these steps, and they receive monthly updates on the status of all Bright Ideas under their supervision. Our program has grown such that we have a part-time Bright Ideas Coordinator whose entire job is to oversee this process, but that certainly was not the case at the beginning. Do not allow technological or personnel hindrances to keep you from beginning your own Bright Ideas program.

Finally, after an idea has been implemented, the supervisor is responsible for recognizing and rewarding the employee whose idea was accepted. We celebrate each individual employee's success, and we also encourage recognition of department- and organization-wide accomplishments. Each of our entities uses different methods for celebrating Bright Idea submission and implementation. A few examples are provided in Figure 7.5.

The following article appeared in our *BHC Daily* training handout, another tool we use to recognize Bright Idea success:

> One of the reasons our organization has a strong mission is so we can have a purpose to keep in front of us every day as employees. Many times in our day-to-day activities it is easy to lose focus. Our mission reminds us to stay on course.
>
> One sign that we are on course is our submission of Bright Ideas, especially cost-saving ones. Maria Sotto, Baptist Health Care Medical Records, submitted a Bright Idea to recycle the chart dividers that

FIGURE 7.5 Celebrating Bright Ideas

- At Jay Hospital, employees receive a gold lapel pen for each implemented idea, and a t-shirt for five implemented ideas.

- At Gulf Breeze Hospital, every two months, the name of each employee with an implemented idea is placed in a drawing for a $50 gift certificate.

- Atmore Community Hospital held a Bright Ideas kickoff at their annual employee picnic. Submitting an idea earned employees the chance to dunk a leader!

- At Baptist Hospital, employees receive gold light bulb-shaped pins for implemented ideas and platinum pins for cost-saving ideas.

- Atmore Community Hospital holds a drawing every three months for employees who have had $1,000 in verified cost-savings ideas.

- D.W. McMillan Memorial Hospital rewards every *submitted* idea with a coupon for a free Dairy Queen sundae.

behavioral medicine and skilled nursing use in their patient care charts. These dividers are usually discarded after the records are microfilmed. Lila McIntyre called the microfilm company and asked if they would be open to our idea of saving and returning our dividers to them for recycling instead of discarding them. This meant that there were more than 5,000 dividers that needed to be reprocessed for use. This daunting task was completed by one of our wonderful volunteers, Dorothy Carden.

Maria, Lila, and Dorothy, thank you for making a difference in our organization. Your idea and teamwork saved us about $700 and gave us a great example of what our mission is all about . . . providing for the customer, being good stewards and working together! Congratulations to each of you for being great stewards of Baptist Health Care's resources.

Are there materials in your department that are being discarded but could be recycled for future use while still providing a safe and quality experience for your customers?

There are tremendous advantages of implementing and developing a Bright Ideas program. The organization benefits by tapping into a powerful source of time-saving, cost-reducing, and service-improving ideas. Employees benefit by having their ingenuity rewarded and their confidence boosted with the knowledge that they have made Baptist Health Care a better organization. Finally, customers benefit from the raised level of service that our Bright Ideas enable us to provide. It's a win–win–win situation, and a powerful tool for motivating and retaining employees.

CHAPTER 8

Celebrating Successes through Reward and Recognition

There are two things people want more than love and money—recognition and praise.

— Mary Kay Ash

We believe she was right.

There is nothing more important to most individuals than knowing that their contributions are valued. Creating a program through which employees' achievements can be consistently recognized fulfills a basic need that exists in all of us to be appreciated for what we do. Not only does it promote an attitude of empowerment, but it also helps retain great employees, nurtures camaraderie, boosts morale, enhances commitment, improves employee satisfaction and—most importantly promotes a workplace that results in happy, satisfied customers.

At Baptist Health Care, we recognize the strong correlation between employee commitment and customer satisfaction. We know that happy, committed employees work more productively and provide better service. By valuing and recognizing our staff, we harness the power of motivation and generate sustained levels of achievement.

Ask any major, successful corporation—from Wal-Mart to Disney—and you'll discover that they have multiple methods of rewarding and recognizing their employees. People are the lifeblood of your organization. When you empower your employees to be partners in your success, they begin to look at their jobs differently. They become team players. They begin to care about the overall reputation of the organization, and consequently, they become the driving force behind change that equals success.

Mark Twain once said, "I can live for a whole year on one compliment." Timely, appropriate recognition has tremendous power in employees' lives, and so, early in our transformation, we sought to develop ways to recognize, reward, and celebrate the right kinds of behaviors.

FIND A REASON TO CELEBRATE

We recognize all employees who make significant contributions to the mission, vision, and values of Baptist Health Care. Employees do things every day that are worthy of praise and recognition, and we as leaders must train ourselves to be alert and aware of opportunities to celebrate achievements. Too many managers believe that their primary job is to find and correct poor performance from an employee. Instead, we encourage our leaders to focus on "catching" their employees doing something right. Positive reinforcement for a job well done can be a much stronger motivator than scolding or punishment.

The opportunities to reward and recognize are endless. We recognize employees for qualities or behaviors such as teamwork, cooperation, communication, and collaboration. We acknowledge behaviors that exceed customer expectations, take initiative, add value to our services, or add a personal touch to their service in support of the WOW! culture. The following list, taken from the *Reward and Recognition Handbook* that we distribute to all of our leaders (see Figure 8.1), suggests common reasons that our employees might receive recognition:

Working short-staffed

Volunteering for overtime when needed

Being a team player

Having a great attitude

Going above and beyond the job description

Exceeding standards

Adding a personal touch

Taking initiative

Creating loyalty

Showing flexibility

Demonstrating creativity

Receiving recognition from a customer

This list is only a starting point. Every employee is unique, and a WOW! culture recognizes these differences and rewards employees for using their own skills and abilities to offer superior service. We encourage our leaders not to wait for a major accomplishment to offer a word of

FIGURE 8.1 Reward and Recognition Handbook

praise; acknowledging the small things that people do to make our organization stand out is one of the best things our leaders can do.

Some rewards and recognitions can be informal and spontaneous. Others can be planned and formally presented. I can offer praise at a department head meeting, in a handwritten thank-you note, or in a quick conversation with an employee in the hallway. The opportunities are there—I just have to take them. So the answer to the question "When should I recognize and reward?" is "As often as possible!"

KNOW YOUR PEOPLE

We understand that people are different, and that every individual wants to be recognized differently. While one person may relish the limelight of group praise, another may shrink in embarrassment at being singled out in a gathering of peers. With this in mind, rule number one is for our leaders to know their employees inside and out. They must learn what makes each individual feel good before they can reward them effectively.

To help our leaders become familiar with each person's preferences, we have developed a tool called the *Reward and Recognition Motivation Assessment*. Given as part of our Traditions orientation, this assessment allows employees to rank, on a scale of one to five, our most common reward methods, including private and public words of praise, WOW awards, and employee of the month recognition. It also asks them to list their favorite candy bar, restaurant, pizza topping, soft drink, and junk food. Following Traditions, each employee's assessment is delivered to his or her department leader so that the leader will be ready when he catches that employee doing something right (see Figure 8.2).

Recently, one of our affiliates, Jay Hospital, was the first facility within Baptist Health Care to reach its annual goal of implemented Bright Ideas. The very next day at their department head meeting, Administrator Mark Faulkner passed out candy bars to each of the department leaders, thanking them for their efforts in achieving this goal. Giving a 50¢ candy bar to a leader doesn't sound terribly meaningful. What made it special for these leaders is that each candy bar happened to be the leader's favorite candy bar. Because Mark had made the effort to keep track of each leader's personal preferences, he was able to personalize the reward for each individual. Meaningful recognition doesn't have to be expensive or time-consuming, but it does have to be geared toward your employees' preferences.

FIGURE 8.2 Employee Profile Worksheet Example

Name _____

Reward and Recognition Motivation Assessment

Please circle the response that best describes your feeling about each of the reward and recognition ideas listed below. Then complete the sentences below.

	None	Minimal	Neutral	Important	Very Important
1. Verbal words of thanks given privately					
2. Verbal recognition given publicly					
3. Written note of appreciation					
4. WOW or STAR award					
5. Certificates of appreciation					
6. Employee of the month recognition					
7. Champion or Legend recognition					
8. Gift certificate					
9. Team celebration					
10. Recognition in the Banner, Centerlines, Board Briefs, etc.					

I came to work at Baptist Health Care because _____

I stay at Baptist Health Care because _____

My favorite candy bar is _____

My favorite lunch restaurant is _____

My favorite pizza topping is _____

My favorite soft drink/juice is _____

My favorite junk food is _____

RECOGNIZE OUTSTANDING
INDIVIDUALS

Once we know how our staff members prefer to be rewarded, we are ready to begin acknowledging outstanding performance. Reward and recognition has become such an integral part of our WOW! culture that we have developed numerous formal award systems for acknowledging superior performance. Here are some of the ways we reward individuals for stellar service:

WOW Super Service Certificates. A WOW award is given to recognize superior service that is directly associated with the pillars of operational excellence. It acknowledges behavior that goes beyond what is expected. We give these awards to employees who exceed customers' expectations, and we also give employees the privilege of recognizing their coworkers by giving WOW awards. Any employee can fill out a WOW certificate. When a person has accumulated five WOW awards, they can be redeemed for a $20 gift certificate to the gift shop or a $15 gift certificate good at local merchants. Copies of the five WOW forms are also placed in the employee's personnel file so that they will be available at evaluation time (see Figure 8.3).

New Employee Cards. Employees who have been part of the Baptist Health Care staff for 90 days receive a card recognizing their contribution to the team. The card is personalized with a photo of the department's employees, signed by each team member, and then presented to the new employee at a department meeting or in an impromptu gathering of coworkers. It is a small but meaningful way to tell new team members, "We're glad you're here. You're welcome and important to us, and we're working hard to assure your success."

One-Year Appreciation Awards. After a year of service, employees receive an appreciation certificate and a one-year gold pin to wear on their uniforms as a symbol of this important career milestone. The pins are distributed to the employee's leader in the month prior to the anniversary.

Multiyear Service Awards. We also celebrate with employees who reach their five-year, ten-year, and fifteen-year milestones. A monthly e-mail alerts department heads and administration of upcoming employee anniversaries, and employees then receive a letter from the president thanking them for their service and inviting them to the quarterly awards ceremony. I present awards to these individuals at a ceremony attended by their leaders and peers. We try to ensure that all departments are well-represented so that the message—the high value of long-term service contributions—is

Figure 8.3 WOW Award Sample

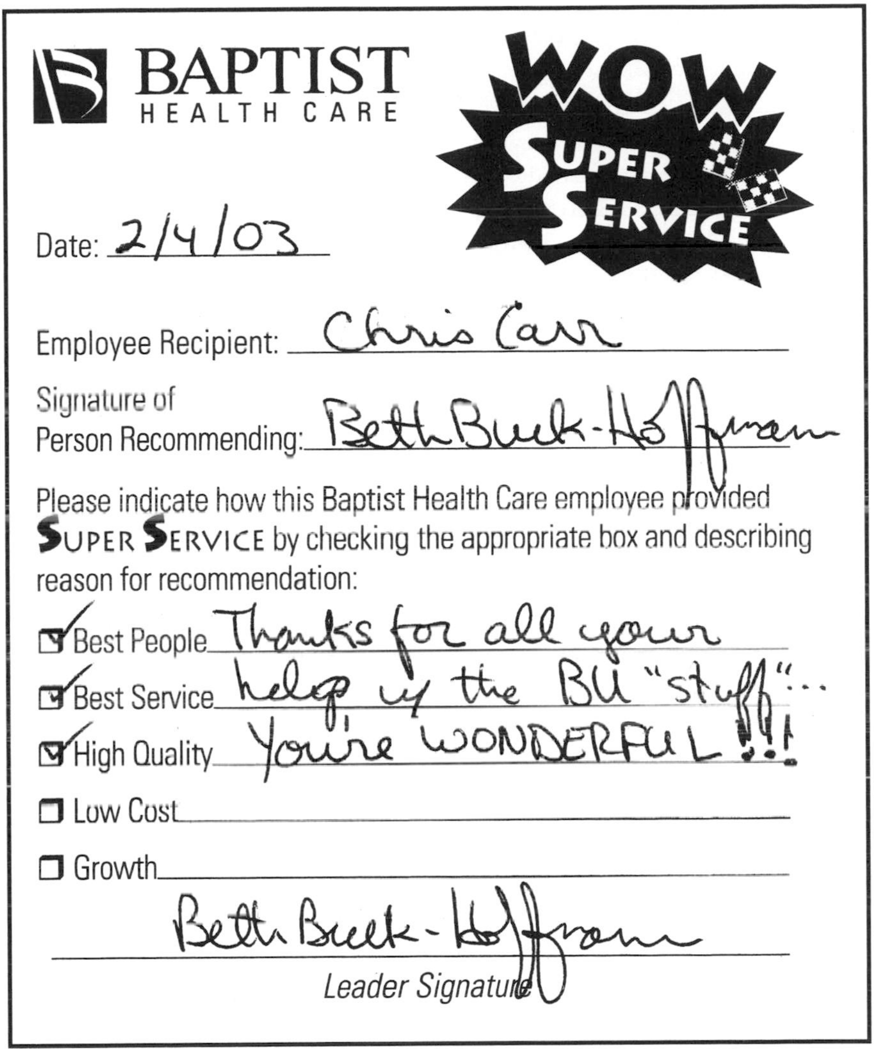

BAPTIST HEALTH CARE

WOW SUPER SERVICE

Date: 2/4/03

Employee Recipient: Chris Carr

Signature of Person Recommending: Beth Buck-Hoffman

Please indicate how this Baptist Health Care employee provided SUPER SERVICE by checking the appropriate box and describing reason for recommendation:

☑ Best People Thanks for all your

☑ Best Service help w/ the BU "stuff"...

☑ High Quality You're WONDERFUL!!!

☐ Low Cost

☐ Growth

Beth Buck-Hoffman

Leader Signature

communicated clearly. Staff members who have surpassed the ten-year service mark receive a letter from me each year in appreciation of their continued service. Employees who have served twenty years or more are also recognized and celebrated at an annual awards luncheon. In these days of high turnover and mobility, we want our employees to know that we appreciate their ongoing commitment to our organization.

Employee of the Month Recognition. Employees who consistently live the values, mission, and standards of Baptist Health Care and help achieve success in our Pillars of Operational Excellence will be recognized by their peers as role models. Leaders can nominate such employees to be recognized as employee of the month. Once selected, the honored employee is surprised by the hospital administrator, who comes to his or her department to present the award and participate in a small celebration reception. The employee also receives a $50 Wal-Mart gift card, a certificate, an employee of the month pin, a special parking space for a month, and a photo posting in the hospital. At the yearly awards ceremony, the twelve employees of the month are recognized and one is chosen as the employee of the year.

Champions. In cases where performance is so exceptional that WOW awards seem inadequate, individuals are recognized as *Champions.* Baptist Health Care Champions are ordinary people who have done extraordinary things for our organization; they have exhibited exemplary behavior or performed specific deeds to help our community, patients, patients' family members, coworkers or our organization. Champions are nominated and selected quarterly. Their leaders present their awards at a department head meeting. Champions are mentioned in the *BHC Daily,* receive a framed plaque, and have their picture posted on a special bulletin board.

Each month we recognize two or three Champions at a board meeting. The employees and their managers attend the meeting, and the managers share their stories with the board members. The board applauds, and the board chairperson thanks the employees for making a difference. It takes only five minutes, but what a powerful message it sends. The employees are sometimes scared to death to come into that boardroom, but when they leave, the positive message ripples through the organization, and they "float" back to their units. Here are just a few examples of actual Champion stories:

> One story tells of a maintenance man who discovered that a patient who was going home had no wheelchair access to his home. This man took it on himself to assess the need, purchase the materials, and go to the patient's home on the weekend to build a wheelchair ramp to meet this patient's need.
>
> Another story tells of a nurse who was caring for a concerned couple. Since the husband was going into surgery that night, they were going to miss their favorite TV show, and the couple was distraught about it. The nurse went home and personally video taped the show, and then

hand-delivered it to the patient's room the next day, telling him that they could watch it as soon as he got well enough.

Another Champion story tells of a cashier who discovered that a certain patient (who was hospitalized for several weeks) had nobody to wash her clothes. This cashier took it upon herself to gather the patient's clothes and wash them for her.

Once, one of our administrators became aware of a terminally ill patient who loved to fish and wanted to go fishing just one more time. This administrator took it upon himself to connect with the patient's doctors and EMS and arrange for an ambulance to take him out to the Pensacola Beach Fishing Pier so that he could fish one last time. The patient died three weeks later.

Legends. Once a year we recognize the most outstanding employees from our list of Champions as *Legends of Baptist Health Care*. These Legends are presented to the members of our nine boards during our annual two-day retreat. We choose ten to twelve Legends each year, including at least one person from each facility and several from our larger entities. Legends and their guests travel by limousine to the retreat, where they dine with the administrator of their facility. A special video presentation showcases each Legend's story, and they receive a framed certificate and special pin. This outstanding group of employees is then applauded enthusiastically by the 200 board members and administrators in the room. We also publish all of their stories in a booklet that we distribute at the retreat and make available at each of our entities after the event. We take out a full-page newspaper ad just to tell our Legend stories; we want to make our community aware of the caliber of employees we have at Baptist Health Care. Here are two of my favorite Legend stories:

Jennifer Brown, a registered nurse at Atmore Community Hospital, is known for bringing joy and comfort to her patients during difficult times.

When she learned that the electricity had been turned off at one of her patients' homes, Jennifer became that patient's advocate, raising money to pay the power bill and assuming responsibility for having service reconnected.

Another inpatient with a terminal illness desperately wanted to see the movie *Pearl Harbor*. Jennifer and a coworker went to great lengths to legitimately obtain a copy of the movie, which at the time had shown in the theater, but had not yet been released on video. Unfortunately, the patient passed away on the evening when the movie was to be shown.

At Christmas, she and coworkers purchase gifts and deliver them to needy families. She has frequently delivered pans of hot cheese biscuits or books to long-stay patients.

She volunteers to help coworkers whenever needed, working extra shifts, making phone calls, completing paperwork, or filling in as house supervisor. Her tireless, selfless spirit and commitment to the patients she serves makes Jennifer Brown a *Legend* of Baptist Health Care.

Another of our Legends performed several acts of kindness for a single patient:

Tony Whitmer, an RN at Baptist Hospital, was able to bond with a patient who was dealing with the effects of a lengthy, life-changing illness.

The patient was in for a long stay, and Tony got a computer set up in the patient's room to help him perform some work and more enjoyably pass the time during his stay.

After the patient was finally discharged to return home, Tony dropped by to check on him and realized that the patient's home was in total disarray following his lengthy hospitalization. His refrigerator no longer worked and was infested with insects. Tony and his son moved the appliance outside and cleaned it thoroughly. Spending his own money, Tony purchased some groceries for the patient and kept the food iced down while the refrigerator drained and dried. Returning the next day, he discovered that the refrigerator still did not work—the infestation had shorted the wiring. Tony explained the situation to coworkers, who took up a collection to buy a new refrigerator. They contacted two employees in Plant Operations, who managed to find a good refrigerator that was donated to the patient. The employees used the money they had collected to purchase more groceries for the man.

Tony Whitmer cared and made a special effort to improve the quality of this patient's life, during and after his hospital stay, and is a *Legend* of Baptist Health Care.

These are the kind of stories we celebrate every year. We all have those stories. Things like that happen in your organization, too, but what do you do with them? How do you celebrate your employees? How do you encourage more of those kinds of behaviors? That's what the Champions and Legends celebrations are all about. By telling and publishing the stories of our Champions and Legends, we show all of Pensacola what makes the Baptist Health Care culture unique, and we inspire and encourage our most dedicated workers. To this day, Bette Harriman, who was recognized as one of our very first Legends, carries the Legend booklet with her story in her purse, eagerly sharing it with anyone who will listen.

Handwritten thank-you notes. One of our most powerful forms of recognition is the practice of sending handwritten thank-you notes to the homes of employees who excel. Being acknowledged away from the workplace, among family and friends, means a great deal to most people. We ask all senior leaders and department heads to acknowledge employees' progress, achievements, or outstanding behavior with a handwritten note. We believe so strongly in the power of thank-you notes that we track them. Each leader has a target number of notes to write each month, and we keep track of how many they have sent and which employees have received them. In our high-speed, e-mail-driven society, employees are touched and honored to know that one of their leaders took the time to write them a personal note of gratitude. This is a wonderful way to build loyalty within a team and throughout the organization.

In his five years with us, John Heer developed a great system for getting his thank-you notes written. He systematically asked various department heads to send him the names of employees who should be recognized along with a two- or three-sentence explanation of what the employee had done to deserve recognition. When his assistant received the names, she addressed an envelope to the employee's home and attached a blank note along with the description of the accomplishment. John took ten to fifteen of those notes home every weekend and got them written and sent out in about thirty minutes. That translates to over 500 employees a year who received a handwritten note from their hospital president at their home. Wow!

That may seem like a simple, inconsequential thing, but you should hear the stories our people tell of what that means to many of our employees who have never received any kind of recognition—much less a handwritten note from the president of their hospital. The son of an employee called John's office one day to tell him how much a thank-you note had meant to his mother. After taking the note to church to show her friends, this employee took her family to Wal-Mart to buy a frame so that she could hang the note on her living room wall. We've heard other stories of employees putting their notes on their refrigerators so that their children can see them. Hand-written thank-you notes have a personal touch that speaks volumes to employees about their value to their leaders and to the organization.

I also know of instances where cards of praise and appreciation have been sent not to our employees, but to their spouses or family members. Sending a thank-you note to a wife whose husband has recently worked overtime or somehow exceeded his job expectations—and thanking her for supporting and encouraging him—can reinforce our WOW! culture to an entire family (see Figure 8.4).

Spontaneous, Informal Recognition. In addition to the formal recognition programs I've listed above, we encourage leaders to find creative ways to make reward and recognition a regular part of their day. We share this list of suggestions with our leaders to spark their own creativity in finding ways to celebrate superior service:

Ways to Recognize an Outstanding Employee

Send a note or e-mail about the person to his or her reporting senior

Mention at a department meeting or in a newsletter

Breakfast items such as doughnuts, pastries, and fruit

A pizza lunch

Departmental employee of the month or quarter

Flowers, balloons, or candy

Letters of praise posted in a suitable place

A photo and comment on your own "Wall of Fame" picture board

A personal phone call

A thank-you note to the family of the employee during periods of increased overtime

A team cookout

A day named after an employee

Recognition buttons

A featured profile on your web site

A "Caught You Doing Something Great Award"

An award you create yourself, even if it's written on the back of your business card

FIGURE 8.4 Handwritten Thank-you Note Sample

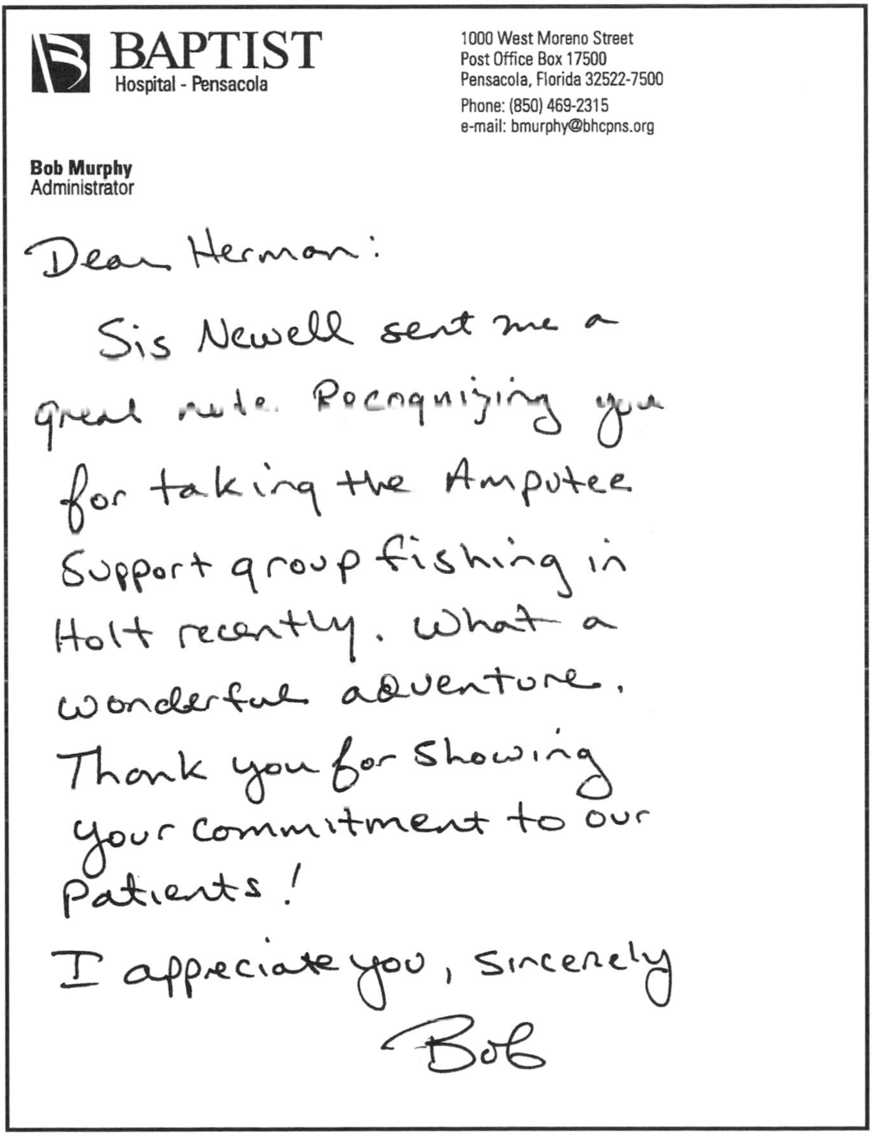

BAPTIST
Hospital - Pensacola

1000 West Moreno Street
Post Office Box 17500
Pensacola, Florida 32522-7500

Phone: (850) 469-2315
e-mail: bmurphy@bhcpns.org

Bob Murphy
Administrator

Dear Herman:

Sis Newell sent me a great note. Recognizing you for taking the Amputee Support group fishing in Holt recently. What a wonderful adventure. Thank you for showing your commitment to our Patients!

I appreciate you, Sincerely

Bob

CELEBRATE TEAM ACHIEVEMENTS

While we devote much of our time and resources to recognizing individual achievements, we also understand the value of team celebrations. We apply the same principles of reward and recognition to every level of our organization. When a service team reaches a goal, we want them to celebrate it. When a department performs beyond expected levels, they deserve to be recognized. And when Baptist Health Care receives an award or recognition or achieves a milestone, we want every single employee to take part in celebrating our success (see Figure 8.5).

One example of team recognition is our traveling weekly patient satisfaction trophy. Each Thursday afternoon, when our patient satisfaction scores are reported, the results are evaluated and the department with the highest inpatient satisfaction results for that week receives the trophy. The trophy travels to a new location each Thursday, unless of course the same department wins repeatedly. For several weeks, the trophy stayed in food services, but eventually another department beat them out. This little dose of competition between departments encourages team loyalty and benefits our customers by raising the level of service that they receive.

Not all group achievements will be recognized by higher levels of leadership. We encourage departments and teams to celebrate their accomplishments as frequently as they have opportunity and not to wait for administration to tell them to party. We want celebration to be a natural part of our environment, and that takes planning and intentionality.

Our teams don't have to look too hard to find reasons to reward themselves. Possible reasons for celebration may include anniversaries, completed group projects, raised patient satisfaction scores, or achievement of target goals. These celebrations can occur spontaneously or as a planned event. They may take place during or after work hours, in staff or committee meetings, or at retreats, hospital functions or department head meetings. Some examples of group and organization-wide celebrations that have been held at our facilities are:

Baptist Hospital's Lab Director encourages open communication by hosting a monthly lunch for six or seven people in his department. He provides drinks and sandwiches and creates an environment that shows his team that he is interested in them. The luncheon is also an opportunity to recognize staff members for their achievements.

FIGURE 8.5 Organization-wide Celebrations Sample

First Rehab spent time outside of work creating a power-point presentation called "This Is Your Life" to celebrate their twenty-fifth anniversary. Team members volunteered to collect funny stories, testimonials, and more!

Health Source Call Center has a monthly "food with a theme day" to celebrate success and build relationships. They decorate, wear costumes, and bring pot-luck dishes.

Jay Hospital recently celebrated their sixteenth consecutive quarter (fourth full year) ranking in the top one percent in patient satisfaction. To celebrate, they planned a "Sweet 16" celebration. They used a birthday party theme, serving hamburgers, hot dogs, cake, and ice cream. During the celebration, Administrator Mark Faulkner popped out of a paper cake to deliver a thank-you speech highlighting his employees' amazing accomplishments.

Gulf Breeze Hospital has used a Mardi Gras theme in numerous celebrations through the years. "Let the Good Times Roll" and "Louisiana Hurricane Party: Taking Patient Satisfaction By Storm" have been catch phrases for these special events. The celebration menu features a crawfish boil and King Cake, and a guest chef from New Orleans engages diners in Cajun banter and makes the rounds from table to table demonstrating the proper technique for consuming crawfish. Food services staff members don Mardi Gras hats and decorative aprons, and moon pies and beads are given to participants. One such celebration incorporated a departmental competition for the design of mini-Mardi Gras floats to use as table decorations. The Cardiopulmonary Department's "Krewe of Rhythms and Sounds" was one of the many prize winning entries.

Gulf Breeze Hospital also makes an effort to thank food service workers for the extra work they put into celebration events for the entire hospital team. Once a year, food service staff members are treated as guests to their own special celebration with a catered menu from an eatery of their choice. This meal is served by hospital leaders, and all leaders are encouraged to drop by to offer personal words of appreciation to these dedicated employees.

REWARD AND RECOGNIZE
PHYSICIANS, TOO

We have found that these principles of reward and recognition apply at every level of our organization, even to those who are not technically our employees. With any individual, if you reward and recognize the kinds of behaviors that you want repeated, you have a better chance of seeing more of those behaviors. Doctors, just like any other employee, desire and deserve to be recognized and rewarded for their contributions and achievements. By finding ways to celebrate their achievements, we keep them feeling like a part of our organization, which benefits everyone, most importantly, our patients.

Whether we are dealing with a single physician with a staff of five or a large practice of doctors with twenty employees, using our reward and recognition practices helps us to acquire and retain the kind of people who will be an asset to us and our patients. We use many of the same types of recognition that we use with other staff—thank you notes, WOW awards, even an occasional Champion recognition. Some of the methods we have used to recognize our physicians are:

Family events (such as a Physician Appreciation Night at the IMAX theater)

Doctor's Day luncheons with gifts

Leadership Retreats (sometimes including their families)

New physician orientation

Physician "mingling" (to welcome and introduce new physicians)

Press releases or newspaper articles to highlight outstanding physicians

WOW awards

Thank you letters to physicians who are mentioned by name on patient surveys

Christmas luncheons for physicians and their staff

Birthday cards from administration

Cookie baskets to department chairs for their hard work

Recognition of accomplishments on our Web site

One-year anniversary recognition

Our employee morale measures testify more powerfully than I ever could to the power of rewarding and recognizing employees. By creating a system that gives leaders frequent and varied opportunities to reward employees for superior service, we have achieved and maintained the highest level of positive morale that our consultants have ever measured. It will work for you, too. You cannot achieve the second key to operational excellence—Select and Retain Great People—without a relentless, consistent commitment to rewarding your employees. They must be reminded frequently that they are valued members of your organization. When this happens, they will in turn reward you by becoming the quality workforce that you need to take your organization to the next level.

KEY THREE

COMMIT
TO SERVICE
EXCELLENCE

Erlene Henderson, a CNA at Jay Hospital, became aware that one of her patients lacked basic home essentials and that these needs had contributed to the patient's decline in health. Even with limited resources, Erlene took it upon herself to purchase several necessities for the patient's home, including curtains for the windows. She then began checking on the patient at home from time to time—while she was off duty—to make sure that the patient's condition was improving.

Several staff members working in Baptist Hospital's surgical unit decided to do something special for a female patient in her thirties who was diagnosed with permanent blindness just before Christmas. They decided to give her things that would help her use some of her other senses, so they gave her a basket of oranges (to smell and to taste) and a music box with an angel (to hear). There wasn't a dry eye in the room when they gave her the gifts.

This is what we mean by service excellence—acts of kindness and care that so greatly exceed expectations that our customers will never forget them. Stories like these have become commonplace in our organization as we have developed a culture that is committed to service excellence. As we have empowered our employees to provide excellent care, they have surpassed even our expectations, consistently offering world-class service to our customers and their families.

As you implement the first two keys—Create and Maintain a Great Culture and Select and Retain Great Employees—those efforts must be coupled with a commitment to service excellence. In this section, I want to share some of the nuts and bolts of providing superior service to your customers. First, in Chapter 9, Maintaining Quality through Service Teams, I will highlight the important role that service teams have played in our journey. Then, in Chapter 10, Scripting for Superior Service, I will describe our methods and guidelines for scripting a best practice that has revolutionized our service. Finally, in Chapter 11, Developing Rounding and Service Recovery Techniques, I will discuss the value of rounding for maintaining superior service and also explain our procedures for handling service opportunities gone wrong.

CHAPTER 9

Maintaining Quality through Service Teams

> *Individual commitment to a group effort—that is what*
> *makes a **team work**, a company **work**, a society **work**,*
> *a civilization **work***
>
> —Vince Lombardi

In October 1995, I walked out of the board meeting at which I had committed us to reaching the seventy-fifth percentile in patient satisfaction in nine months, went immediately to my office, and dictated a memo—we weren't in the e-mail age yet in 1995—to our leaders and workforce saying, "Go thou and deliver great service!" Overnight our culture was transformed, and we all lived happily ever after.

I don't think so.

An edict from senior management was not the answer to our cultural problems—transformed employees were. If we were going to achieve the monumental change in our culture that we desired, it was going to have to come from our staff. Only they could provide the kind of superior service that is essential to a WOW! culture.

But how do you convince employees to raise their level of service? How do you make them the drivers of your cultural change? We decided to make them responsible for creating the structure that would facilitate continual service excellence. From a management perspective, we did a scary thing: We turned the organization over to the employees.

One of the first things we did as we embarked on our journey in 1995 was to create seven service teams, led by and made up entirely of employees. Each of these teams consisted of ten to twenty-five frontline employees from departments throughout the hospital (amounting to over ten percent of our workforce!), and they were charged with the task of identifying and implementing the necessary steps to make us a national leader in service excellence. The seven original teams were Measurement, Standards, Communication, Linkage, Irritants, Physician, and WOW.

The teams have evolved somewhat over the years as we have moved forward. In the second evolution, we kept the Measurement, Standards, Linkage, and Loyalty teams and added Inpatient, Outpatient, and Physician Satisfaction teams. We recognized that satisfied employees were necessary in order to have satisfied patients or customers and that the two combined created a work environment that would lead to satisfied physicians. In 2001 we established the structure that is still in place today. In this final evolution, we identified the need for five teams: a Culture team (whose role encompassed the responsibilities of the old Measurement and Standards teams), a Communications team (as a result of our recognition of the never-ending need to find new and creative ways to communicate with our workforce and customers), an Employee Loyalty team, a Customer Loyalty team, and a Physician Loyalty team (see Figure 9.1).

FIGURE 9.1 Evolution of Service Teams

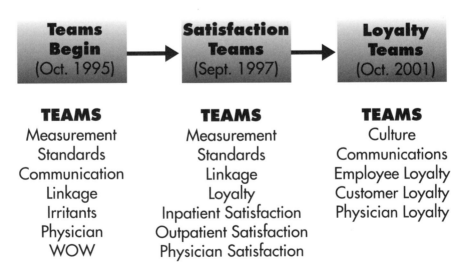

Our transition from using the term "satisfaction" to the term "loyalty" was facilitated by a visit from nationally known motivational speaker and author Jeffrey Gitomer. As our featured guest at a Baptist University quarterly session, he challenged us all. In his book *Customer Satisfaction Is Worthless, Customer Loyalty Is Priceless: How to Make Customers Love You, Keep Them Coming Back and Tell Everyone They Know* (Bard Press, 1998), Gitomer powerfully presents the value of creating customer loyalty. My favorite line from the book is, "Would you rather your spouse be satisfied or loyal?" I don't want my wife to simply be "satisfied," nor do I want that from our employees, customers, and physicians. As we challenged ourselves six years into the journey to continue to raise the bar, we decided to focus on gaining the loyalty of each of these groups, and we asked our service teams to guide us in finding the best ways to do that.

LAYING THE FOUNDATION

In October 1995, when we made the decision to create these teams and empower our employees, we truly had no blueprint showing where we wanted them to take us. We knew from looking in the mirror that we were not satisfied with where we were, and we knew that we needed to engage our entire workforce to hit the lofty targets we had set. I'd like to share a little of the thought process we went through as we developed these teams.

Our senior management team thought carefully about the roles and responsibilities of each team. We asked, "What are the most important characteristics a team needs to have in order to get the results we want?" That led us to the following guidelines as we set up each team:

Remember to Diversify,

Choose Opportunities for Improvement,

Implement Solutions, and

Celebrate!

Remember to Diversify

Healthcare organizations are incredibly diverse. They are diverse in gender (though the usual hospital workforce is typically about eighty percent female), race, educational training, and, certainly, compensation levels. If diversity is important in your organization, the makeup of your service teams must reflect it. Racial and gender balance were not enough for our service teams; we also needed departmental diversity. To gain input from as many segments of your employee population as possible, you must create a team that involves different people with different experiences. Therefore, you must diversify.

Choose Opportunities for Improvement

Second, you must have the teams choose, or take ownership of, opportunities for improvement. After the teams were selected, we described their area of focus and then encouraged them to start with a brainstorming session. This was one of our first attempts to drill into our culture the idea that we wanted more than just our employees' licenses and bodies coming to work everyday, but that we desperately needed them to engage their minds, souls, and spirits in helping us create a different environment. The individual team was a wonderful outlet for new ideas that brought dramatic change to our organization.

Implement Solutions

The third step is to implement solutions. When teams are just getting started, it is important for them, in terms of recognition and prestige, to implement the solution they identify for the given problem. This allows the team to gain authority and respect from other employees in the workforce as their colleagues see the positive outcomes from this process.

Celebrate!

Finally, and most importantly, the teams must celebrate! As revealed in Chapter 8, Celebrating Successes through Reward and Recognition, we have become an organization that loves to party. This is where that emphasis began. When a problem is solved or a function of the organization is improved as a result of a team's effort, it is crucial that they celebrate their success. Some achievements merit an organization-wide celebration while others may require some smaller recognition, but no accomplishment is too small to enjoy.

THE TEAMS TODAY

Today, nine years after we started this journey, our teams are just as active as they were at the beginning. The names have changed as our culture has evolved (and they'll probably change again when the time is right), but throughout the process they have brought us critical focus and enabled us to sustain our world-class results year after year. Let me share with you some of the things these teams have accomplished, and some of the things they are still doing.

Culture Team

Analyze and measure customer satisfaction results and develop and implement actions for improvement.

Guide customer service strategy for service focus.

I like to say that the primary function of the *Culture team* is to make sure that we "keep the main thing the main thing." Established in 2001, this team took on the responsibilities of the original Standards and Measurement teams. Setting standards at every level of the organization and then measuring, measuring, measuring are the primary tasks of this team. We want them to continually remind us to focus on our employees and customers, enabling us to reach our goal of being employer of choice in our industry.

The Culture team exists to establish the standards that define who we are as an organization, and then to put in place mechanisms to measure results so that we can hold ourselves accountable to meet those lofty standards. This team has been a driving force behind our outstanding achievements, for without a great culture, you'll never deliver great service.

In Chapter 6, Selecting the Best Employees, I talked about the standards of performance that our employees developed for Baptist Hospital early in our transformation. I can't emphasize enough the importance of establishing a set of standards that define your expectations for every team member. It was the predecessor to the Culture team, the Standards team, that developed our original standards of performance. The brochure that they developed states, "It is the mission of the Baptist Hospital Standards Team to ensure service excellence and high customer satisfaction by cultivating desirable behaviors among employees." "Cultivating" is a key word in that mission statement. Great vegetables or fruit, great musical talent, and great customer service levels don't just happen. They take years of cultivating, and that is what this team is all about for us—an ongoing cultivation process.

The original Standards team consisted of a dozen or so employees who created a list of performance standards that to this day are upheld by every employee of Baptist Hospital. The team originally put together a list of fifty desirable behaviors, then over a series of weekly meetings worked their way down to the ten standards that best characterize the mission and values of Baptist Health Care.

These standards, as you read in Chapter 6, Selecting the Best Employees, were identified as Attitude, Appearance, Communication, Call Lights, Commitment to Coworkers, Customer Waiting, Elevator Etiquette, Privacy, Safety Awareness, and Sense of Ownership. Since they first presented the standards to our employees, the Standards, now Culture, team has focused on promoting and driving deep into the culture these ten standards of behavior. Every month they invent new and fresh ways to highlight our "standard of the month," using things like banners, activities, and contests to keep them always before us.

The Culture team also creates and supervises other emphases that are important to maintaining the culture of Baptist Health Care. One such emphasis is the designation of October as "Christian Emphasis" month. The Culture team has a Faith-In-Action subcommittee that plans and oversees numerous activities as part of this special emphasis.

The second primary function of the Culture team is to analyze and measure everything that we do with a special emphasis on customer satisfaction. They take our customer satisfaction results and develop implementable action plans for improvement based on the feedback they receive. Our previous practice—which I fear is all too common—had been to take the feedback we received, give it very little attention, and then file it away. As we set our sights on being the best healthcare system in America, we found that we were neglecting a powerful tool for improving our service. We asked the Culture team to take our satisfaction results and break the information down into small, actionable steps that would make us better service providers. They have developed a highly effective system for sharing this information, and today employees in every area of our organization learn very quickly about the measurable data that applies to their department, along with suggested actions for improvement.

Another "measurement" task they perform is to develop actionable summaries of our monthly and quarterly patient satisfaction survey results. Those summaries are then distributed to Department Heads within the hospital with suggestions for improvement and requests for feedback on action steps and timelines for implementation. The Team has been very conscientious in making the reports more reader friendly as requested by employees throughout the hospital.

Lynda Barrett, Director of Planning for Baptist Health Care, describes her experience as leader of this team: "I have been involved with the Culture Team for several years. It has been a wonderful way to keep in touch with the patient care side of our organization even when you are not involved with patients on a day-to-day basis. Our main focus is digging deeper into our [patient satisfaction] results to see where opportunities for improvement are, as well as identifying what we are doing right."

Communication Team

Gather and disseminate information to all staff, and establish and maintain guidelines for the posting of communications throughout the hospital.

One of our original seven teams was a *Communications team*, and in 2004 we still think it is vital to have a Communications team. Why? If we truly believe (and we do!) that we are only as strong as our weakest link, and that our results and our ability to reach the world-class goals that we have set for our organization are dependent on engaging every member of our team, then we must relentlessly look for ways to share with those coworkers where we are headed and how far we have come in achieving those goals.

As part of our "no secrets" environment, the Communications team makes sure that all Baptist employees have access to all of the information that is available to senior management. As stated by the Communications team, "Our purpose is to gather and disseminate information to all staff, and to establish and maintain guidelines for the posting of communications throughout the hospital."

One of the main responsibilities of the Communications team is the continuous publication of the *BHC Daily*, a daily training handout that all of our employees read and discuss in small groups every day. Since its beginnings at Baptist Hospital in 2001, which I described in Chapter 5, Engaging Your Workforce: Communicate, Communicate, Communicate!, the *BHC Daily* has grown to encompass every facility under the Baptist Health Care banner, and the Communications team now assures that each *BHC Daily* is facility-specific. For example, our employees at our newest facility,

Baptist Medical Park, no longer hear about success stories and financial growth at Baptist Hospital; instead, they now learn about their own facility's standards, financials, and achievements. The Communications team works diligently to gather and disseminate all of this information.

Communications Team Leader Eli Pagonis captures the essence of his team's purpose: "Effective communication is a key ingredient to a successful work environment. Without it people merely hear, but with it we listen and grow. It is this ideal that BHC has embraced to offer its employees and staff the opportunity to gain the knowledge necessary to improve the organization, and to enable them to maintain our best practices for all who we serve."

The Communications team also takes responsibility for reinforcing alignment of goals through visual communication within the organization. By approving and monitoring cork strip posting areas, information boards, and elevator displays throughout the facility, they ensure that a standard of quality is controlled and that the data in these areas is current and not six months old.

Employee Loyalty Team

Establish and maintain position as "employer of choice." Recognize and reward employees' achievements through hospital-wide celebrations.

You will never deliver great service unless your workforce takes you there. I can't reinforce that point enough. The *Employee Loyalty team* exists to continuously find ways to engage our workforce in this noble task. "Everyone in the organization is capable of contributing; everyone knows something about their job or the organization as a whole that can be improved. It may seem like a small improvement but a series of those, a continuous series of those, will have a tremendous impact on an organization, provided you have the authority to make changes. The Employee Loyalty team gives us that authority at Baptist," says current Team Facilitator Emily Altazan.

The function of the Employee Loyalty team is to establish and maintain our position as "employer of choice." They seek to accomplish this by recognizing and rewarding employees' achievements through hospital-wide celebrations and by constantly striving to support the staff with resources to enhance their personal growth.

Several years into our journey, we made a conscious decision to always have the People Pillar lead off any discussion or display of the five Pillars.

Why? It was a simple recognition that without the right culture, we could never attain world class results. Where does culture reside? It resides in the hearts and spirits of your workforce. You can set big, hairy, audacious goals all day long, but if you don't engage your workforce, and if they don't buy into those goals, you're wasting your time. How many times have you heard CEOs around the country say, "Our employees are our greatest assets"? I've heard it often. We decided to live it. It is the Employee Loyalty team's responsibility to keep our greatest assets happy and to keep them *here*. As I said earlier, it is my belief that people can be as healthy and as happy at work as they are at home, or even more so. We charged this team to create an environment that made sure our best people, *all* of our people, felt good coming to work and felt good going home from work every day.

The creativity of this team constantly amazes me. Recently, they invited the Pensacola Police Department to conduct two sessions on personal safety awareness. We have a current marketing campaign with the slogan, "You'll like how Baptist cares for you." They played off of that slogan in these sessions, entitling them "You will like how Baptist looks out for you."

Another recent Bright Idea submitted directly to the Employee Loyalty team was to have an employee community shower within the hospital for staff members who walk, jog, or bike to work or during lunch to refresh and feel clean before going to their work unit. The employee in the Bio/Med Department who submitted the idea reminded us that we were promoting, through our "Get Healthy, Pensacola!" initiative, health-conscience programs to members of the community. He suggested that we should be just as diligent in encouraging our own workforce to get healthy. Having a team that never stops looking for ways to encourage, support, and provide for our workforce to show them how much they are appreciated is a priceless commodity.

This Employee Loyalty team, as I mentioned, is constantly looking for opportunities to "celebrate with a purpose." Recently, during National Hospital Week, when we treat our employees to a traditional pancake breakfast, this team used the pancake idea to tell staff that we were "flipping over our latest customer satisfaction scores." Another year, the theme for the pancake breakfast was how Baptist "stacks up" against the competition (see Figure 9.2). Tying positive results to celebratory opportunities does not generally happen without a conscious effort; but it can become second nature in your organization when you have a team that is constantly looking for ways to celebrate, encourage, and recognize positive results.

FIGURE 9.2 Pancake Breakfast Flyer Sample

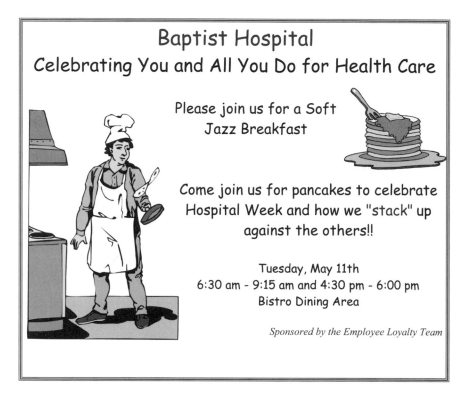

Customer Loyalty Team

To earn customer loyalty today, tomorrow, and into the future. Quality through customer loyalty, satisfaction, and service recovery.

The charge of the Customer Loyalty team is to earn customer loyalty today, tomorrow, and into the future. This team's credo is "quality through customer loyalty, satisfaction, and service recovery." In a healthcare market such as Pensacola, with multiple facilities vying for a larger piece of the market share, it is important that we make a great first impression and keep our customers coming back. Loyalty from customers does not come from delivering average or even expected levels of service. Loyalty comes when our customers get more than they expect or deserve, time after time after time. That's the goal of this team—to help us analyze the data, evaluate the opportunities, and deliver the service that will create loyal, "I'm going to stick with you" customers.

The result of this team's work is woven throughout everything that we do. Therefore, it is intertwined throughout every chapter of this book. In this section, I will share a few examples of the kinds of things that have come from this never-ending, relentless focus on customer loyalty.

Senior management works very closely with this team to make sure that an exceptional employee's good work does not go unnoticed. It may seem out of place to talk about rewarding and recognizing exceptional employees in the *customer loyalty* section, but let me explain. It bears repeating over and over that you can't deliver great service and create loyal customers unless you engage your workforce to take you there. That said, below is an example of a note that is personally signed by the President of Baptist Hospital and mailed to an employee whose name was singled out in a patient satisfaction survey for having delivered great service.

Dear Barrie,

On a recent patient satisfaction survey, your name was mentioned for exceptional performance. The bar is set high at Baptist Hospital, and yet you still exceeded expectations. Thank you for your noteworthy job performance. The Customer Loyalty team, Bob, Mark, Diane, and I congratulate you for contributing positively to the Baptist Health Care culture.

Bob Murphy
Administrator, Baptist Hospital

Every employee mentioned by name in a returned patient satisfaction survey receives a note similar to this one. Do you think that reinforces positive behavior? You bet it does! We want to reward the kind of behavior that will create lifelong, loyal customers.

The Customer Loyalty team is always on the lookout for new services we can create to ensure that customers who choose Baptist as their healthcare provider never want to go elsewhere. For example, at the suggestion of this team, we established a free valet parking service to make our customers' arrival at our facility as smooth and painless as possible. No tipping is allowed as part of this service, and customers are often treated to a free windshield wash and a complimentary key chain.

Another example of going the extra mile is ensuring that inpatients who are celebrating a birthday are adequately recognized. The Customer Loyalty Team sees that a "Happy Birthday!" balloon makes its way to the room of every patient celebrating their special day. Little demonstrations such as this go a long way in ensuring that our patients will again choose Baptist when the need arises, and the Customer Loyalty Team keeps us from letting those opportunities pass us by.

Physician Loyalty Team

Enhance the image of our physicians as competent and well qualified. Enhance physician–hospital collaboration. Enhance patient satisfaction.

When I share our success story around the country, people often want to know how we engaged our physicians. Physician involvement, support, and engagement is a major issue in healthcare today, and I will talk more specifically about our efforts in this area in the Appendix, *What about the Physicians?* However, from day one of our transformation, we have had a Physician Loyalty team looking for opportunities to WOW! our physicians. We understand that these physicians make choices everyday about where to admit their patients.

One thing that the Physician Loyalty team did early on was to identify a list of irritants to our physicians. Once we had identified those areas of frustration, this team began the process of removing them and turning those situations into WOW! events.

Let me share one example of how we transformed an irritant into a WOW! The team determined that one of the greatest irritants to physicians is when they are called out of a busy office practice at 2 P.M. or out of a deep sleep at 2 A.M. by a nurse on the floor who is not armed with the appropriate information. After the nurse had asked a specific question about a patient, the physician would often respond with another question, to which the nurse would reply, "Oh, wait a minute, I have to find the chart." This was understandably irritating to our physicians, whose time is valuable. When I share this story around the country, I see physicians' heads nodding in the audience as they recall how frustrating this can be.

Determined to eliminate this irritant for our physicians, the Physician Loyalty team worked with nursing administration to establish a policy—followed diligently to this day—that our nurses do not call a physician unless they already have a patient's chart in hand. This is one small way that we can demonstrate to our physicians that we care about their time and we are committed to gaining their loyalty. By identifying the problem and working with frontline staff to develop and implement a solution, our Physician Loyalty team turned this common irritant into a WOW! for our physicians.

As long as I am CEO at Baptist Health Care, and I believe long after that, we will continue to have these teams or whatever their successors may be. No matter how our organization grows, we will continue to need a driving focus on culture, a strong commitment to communicate the message, and an unending effort to wow our employees, customers, and physicians. Service teams are the most effective method we have found to keep our employees driving the culture.

CHAPTER 10

Scripting for Superior Service

For me, words are a form of action, capable of influencing change.

—Ingrid Bengis, author

Would you like fries with that?

Will you need a rental car?

For your safety, please return your tray tables to their upright and locked position.

Our practice of scripting puts us in good company. From fast-food restaurants to five star hotels, scripting is an essential business practice for many major corporations. Most of us encounter numerous scripts on a daily basis but may not realize the impact they have on us. By benchmarking companies such as Ritz Carlton and Disney, we've seen the significant effect that consistent scripting has on satisfaction scores. As a customer service initiative, scripting can really set an organization apart from competitors.

WHAT IS SCRIPTING?

When my children were growing up, my wife and I taught them to say, "Yes, ma'am," and "Yes, sir" when talking to adults. We taught them to tell callers, "I'm sorry, he can't come to the phone. May I take a message?"

when we weren't home and to say "Excuse me" when they bumped into someone. By defining the words and behaviors we expected in each of these situations, we increased the chances that our children would send the message we wanted them to send. That is what scripting is all about.

A script is simply a prescribed set of words and behaviors carefully designed to send a message. Scripting ensures that we do all the things we need to do to send a consistent, positive message to our patients and their families. It includes saying the right words, but it is also much more than that. Scripting includes modeling positive body language, maintaining eye contact, smiling, and stopping what you are doing to give full attention to the customer. It is thoughtful, planned communication.

Scripts guide staff to say certain things and act certain ways in given situations—both with patients and with each other. They do *not* require robotic, verbatim delivery of an insincere message, but rather a personalized communication with a predetermined meaning. They are designed not to restrict our employees, but to free them to provide the most effective service possible. Scripting encourages the behaviors and words that will be most meaningful to the people we serve.

At Baptist Health Care, each department has its own individualized scripts based on the regular interactions that those employees have with customers. In addition to those, we also have organization-wide scripts that our employees are expected to use. Our three most famous scripts are: (1) "May I take you where you're going?"; (2) "Is there anything else I can do for you? I have the time."; and (3) "How can I make this better for you?" We believe so strongly in the value of all of our employees using these scripts that we teach them as part of Traditions. Before new employees ever report to their departments for work, they have already learned to communicate these three messages, and they are accountable for doing so.

WHY SCRIPT?

There are numerous reasons to script the key interactions between your customers and your people. Most importantly, scripting allows for consistency of message across the organization. It prevents customers from hearing conflicting messages from different employees during their stay, and it allows us to be sure that all of the important things that need to be done or said in key interactions are included. Our patients are impressed when every employee who visits their room communicates the same message of care, concern, and willingness to help. Our patient satisfaction scores verify the impact of this consistency, which we achieve by faithfully using our scripts.

A good script can be critical in changing customer attitudes. Using the right words can make the difference between a disgruntled customer and a satisfied one. For example, inconvenience issues arise in every hospital. No one likes to wait for an appointment, test, or treatment, but these delays cannot always be avoided. What can make a difference, however, is the message we deliver at the time of the inconvenience. A simple acknowledgement of the delay and offer to help can speak volumes to a customer. We teach our employees to say, "I realize it may take a while for the doctor to see you. Is there anything I can do to help with the inconvenience?" Even if the patient doesn't need anything (which is often the case), the employee has communicated concern for the patient's needs and appreciation of their patience. This can make all the difference in the way a customer feels about our service.

And customers who feel better about our service will be more likely to rate us higher on our patient satisfaction surveys. Another advantage to scripting is that it can contribute to positive survey results by correlating directly to satisfaction surveys. For example, one of the questions on our survey asks, "Did you experience very good patient service?" We have found that by adding the statement, "We want to be sure you experience very good patient service here at our hospital" to employee scripts, we can increase the positive responses to that question. This is only effective if staff members have bought in to using scripts; when that happens, every employee that a patient encounters will send the same consistent message— through their words *and* actions—that we are striving to provide excellent service.

Scripting can also be quite advantageous in handling difficult situations. Many of our employees have shared how grateful they were to have a set of words and behaviors in mind when they found themselves dealing with a difficult patient or patient's family member. In interactions with unhappy customers, it is vital that employees send the right message, and having a plan laid out ahead of time makes it much easier for these employees—who may be flustered or offended by a customer's comments or behavior—to continue to provide superior service.

Finally, scripting can be valuable when we have disappointed a customer and need to conduct service recovery. We don't believe we have lost the opportunity to gain a satisfied customer if something unpleasant

FIGURE 10.1 Scripting Advantages

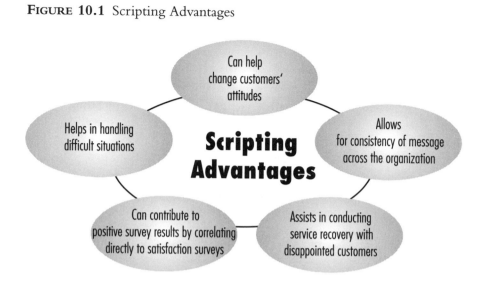

happens during their stay. On the contrary, some of our most vocally and visibly loyal customers are those who have had a negative experience turned around. With this in mind, we carefully develop service recovery scripts to allow us to make the most of this delicate opportunity. Statements like, "We clearly did not meet your expectations. How can I make this better?" and "I am sorry for your experience. That is not the way we like for things to be here at Baptist Hospital. I will take care of this personally" can transform unhappy, dissatisfied customers into radically loyal ones. This is the power of scripting (see Figure 10.1).

WHEN SHOULD I SCRIPT?

The first step to developing effective scripts for your organization is to identify the moments of truth that your customers experience. We define a moment of truth as any contact that the customer has with the organization that provides an opportunity for the customer to form an impression—positive or negative. Moments of truth are critical junctures in a customer's encounter with your organization that will color his or her entire experience. Scripting enables us to do all we can do to ensure that these interactions produce positive results. Figure 10.2 demonstrates some of the ways we ask our employees to turn negative encounters into positive ones.

To identify moments of truth in your organization, think through the entire experience that a customer would have using the services you provide. In any organization, customers go through a continuous sequence of events, all with the potential to create lasting impressions. For us, some of

FIGURE 10.2 Re-framing Communication with Scripting: Turning Negatives into Positives

Instead of . . .	*Say . . .*
"No, I don't have the time."	"Yes! I can help you in five minutes."
"We're short staffed."	"We may be busy, but we're never too busy to help you!"
"I don't know."	"I think I can help you find the answer."
"I can't do that."	"Consider it done."
"That's not my patient."	"I'll go with you and we can do it together."
"It's Nursing's fault and I can't believe they haven't helped you yet."	"I'm sorry that happened. What can I do to help?"
"No."	"No problem."
"It's your job to get the patient up."	"I'd be happy to teach you so next time you won't have any trouble."
"I have a problem."	"I have a solution to a problem."

the key times to use scripting include: clinical procedures, telephone conversations, interactions in patient rooms, exchanges with physicians, and encounters with patients in hallways or the parking lot. All of these are moments of truth.

Some staff members may have an obvious need for scripts, such as nurses who make daily rounds to patient rooms or regular discharge phone calls to patients, while others, like housekeeping or food service workers, may not immediately see the need to standardize their actions. But consistency is only achieved when every member of the workforce chooses to convey the same message. Every employee who has any interaction with customers should have some sort of script defining acceptable words and behaviors.

HOW DO I WRITE A SCRIPT?

Once you have identified the moments of truth that require scripted behaviors, you must decide what message you want your employees to send in each of those interactions. We teach our employees to follow these four steps in writing meaningful scripts:

1. Identify the need. This step includes asking what the customer wants or needs *and* what we want or need as service providers. In other words, what is the goal of the script? What is the desired outcome? It may be to create a certain impression, provide an explanation, or to ease concerns or fears—the possibilities are endless. How do you know what messages you need to send to customers? By *listening* to them—and to your employees. Use your customer satisfaction survey results to determine what needs are not being adequately met, and begin by developing scripts that will help in those situations.

EXAMPLE

We learned that patients in our Emergency Department did not understand why the curtains were pulled around their beds. Some felt that this act isolated them from the very doctors and nurses who were there to help them, while others felt that it was to prevent them from watching other patients. We identified a need for understanding; we needed our patients to understand that the main reason the curtains were pulled was for their own privacy.

---

2. Determine the key words for the script. This step can be crucial to the effectiveness of the script. Your choice of words matters, and you must determine what key words or phrases will be the most meaningful to your customers. From the customer's point of view, what concepts or key ideas are most important to them as they interact with you? What are the hot button issues? Choose words that will directly address your customers' concerns.

EXAMPLE

The key word that our customers needed to hear as we drew the curtain around them was "privacy." They needed to know that concern for their privacy—not a desire to isolate or hide from them was the motivation behind our employees' behavior.

3. Write the script. Once you have identified the key words, the script will practically write itself. We teach our employees to ask two questions when writing scripts: First, what should we say or ask? Second, what should we do? Identifying appropriate behavior is an essential step in script writing; the behavior must accompany the words in order for your employees to send the message you desire in a consistent, caring way.

EXAMPLE

We developed the script, "I'm pulling the curtain to protect your privacy" and asked employees to use it every time they pull the curtain around a patient.

4. Practice and implement the script. The transition to using scripted interactions can be difficult for some employees. Even for those who adapt quickly, practice can make them more effective in delivering meaningful messages. When we teach scripting, we encourage employees to partner up and role play different scripted situations so that they will see what it feels like to use those words.

Let me emphasize again that we don't ask our employees to be robotic, spouting out predetermined messages with little feeling or sincerity. This

FIGURE 10.3 Four Steps in Writing Meaningful Scripts

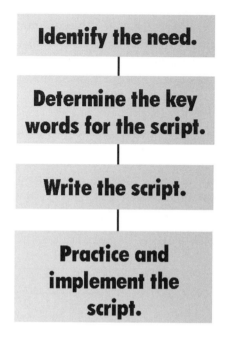

type of scripting can be ineffective and detrimental to a customer's opinion of your organization. We expect and encourage our employees to personalize their scripts with smiles or other appropriate facial expressions, body language, tone of voice, and eye contact. We want them to make the messages their own and share them in a way that works for them (see Figure 10.3).

HOW DO I TEACH MY EMPLOYEES TO SCRIPT?

We have discovered that the key to implementing effective scripting is to incorporate it into daily routines. It must be a consistent, regular part of the culture in order for employees to truly embrace it. We begin to teach scripting as soon as new employees join our team; before they leave orientation, they have learned our three most common scripts and practiced using them with each other. If an employee leaves Traditions and sees a visitor in the hallway who looks lost, we expect him or her to ask that person, "May I take you where you're going?" By communicating early in the process that scripting is important to us, we increase the chances that employees will eagerly embrace the practice themselves.

Once employees have learned their scripts and begun their daily routines, we must continue to reinforce the value and benefits of scripting in as many different and creative ways as we can. One way we do this is by frequently addressing scripting issues in our daily communication tool, the *BHC Daily*. We roll out new scripts and discuss scripting concerns in regular department communication meetings, giving employees a chance to offer feedback and suggestions. We also occasionally hold contests and offer prizes for improved or new scripts, encouraging employees to help us make our scripts as effective as possible. The Bright Ideas program and reward systems I described in Chapters 7, Maximizing Employee Loyalty, and 8, Celebrating Successes through Reward and Recognition, can also be used to encourage scripting. Script improvements qualify as Bright Ideas, making employees with implementable suggestions eligible for rewards through the Bright Ideas program. We hold our leaders accountable for promoting scripting in their departments, and we are sure to celebrate when scripting accounts for a rise in patient satisfaction scores.

Using scripting consistently is the key to getting consistent results. See that your employees are sufficiently trained, and then inspire them to use the tools they have received. It *will* make a difference. Consider this example of the power that scripting can have:

An RN from another state had heard about Baptist Hospital through her previous employer. That hospital had benchmarked Baptist Health Care and attended our monthly Baptist Leadership Institute seminar. When the RN moved to Pensacola, she applied to work at Baptist Hospital based on what she had heard. She also applied to work at the other hospitals in town, but she chose to come to Baptist Hospital because of her first impression on our campus. When she arrived and was obviously lost, a security officer approached her and said, "You look lost. Can I take you where you're going?" It was at that point that she realized that all the things we say we do at Baptist Health Care really happen.

In this case, scripting made a difference not only to our customers, but to a future employee. How motivated do you think that this RN was to use scripting herself when she had already experienced its effectiveness? I doubt that we had a hard time convincing her to use our scripts.

SAMPLE SCRIPTS

Here are some examples of scripts that we have found effective:

When a patient says I'm sorry to bother you:

"Of course you're not a bother . . ."

When taking a blood sample early in the morning:

"Your physician cares about you very much, so he has asked that we get a blood sample very early so the results can be posted on the chart by the time he makes rounds in the morning."

When there are questions about parking:

"We have free parking assistance. If you pull your car under the covered entrance, we'll park your car for you."

When a patient asks a question during a test or treatment:

"I'm glad you asked that . . ." and respond with information. The more knowledgeable the patient is, the more likely he or she will be to cooperate.

When the noise level is high in and around a room:

"Our patients are resting. Can you please help us to keep it quiet? Thank you."

When a patient says, "Oh, just one more thing . . .":

Take your hand off the door, step toward the patient and listen attentively.

When you sense that a patient is ill at ease:

"I realize that being away from home is inconvenient. Is there something I can do to help, such as making a call for you or getting you a phone book, paper, and pen?"

When you sense a need to comfort a patient during a test or treatment:

"For your comfort, I am giving you this warm blanket."

And to the patient's family member:

"We want to make (patient's name) as comfortable as possible. Please let us know if you observe that he or she is not."

In addition to the many one- or two-line scripts that our employees use, we have also developed more involved scripts for regular patient-customer interactions such as admission to the hospital, medical procedures, and service recovery. Our phlebotomists use the following script when visiting a patient's room to draw blood:

1. Enter the room with a smile on your face. Be happy.
2. Always knock before entering and greet your patient by name.
3. Clearly state your name, the department and why you are there.

   "Hi, Mrs. Jones, I am Joe Smith from the Laboratory and your doctor has ordered some blood tests on you and I am here to draw your blood."

4. Don't forget to check the armband, and follow all safety guidelines.
5. Explain step-by-step the procedure you are doing and inform the patient that the stick may be painful.

   "Mrs. Jones, I need to turn on your light. Is that all right with you?"

   "I am going to place a tourniquet around your arm. If the tourniquet is too tight or painful, please let me know."

   "I am cleaning off your arm. Now I am going to draw your blood and you may feel a sharp stick." (You may use "big stick," "quick stick," or whatever you feel comfortable saying as long as you emphasize that they may experience some pain.)

   "I'm finished getting all the blood that is required for the blood test and I am now withdrawing the needle and placing a piece of gauze over the site. Will you please assist me in holding pressure on the site?" (If the patient is unable to hold pressure, you must hold the pressure.)

   "I am going to place a bandage on the site. Are you allergic to any tape? You may take the tape off in five minutes."

6. While drawing the patient's blood or immediately after drawing the blood, the phlebotomist should ask questions about the service he or she has been experiencing.

"Are you happy with the meals you are being served?"

"Is the cleanliness of your room up to your satisfaction?"

"Are the television, remote, and bed functioning properly?" (If the patient answers any of these questions negatively, while standing in the patient's room the phlebotomist should call and report the problem immediately.)

7. Give the patient the option of having his or her light left on or off. Return the tray table to within the patient's reach. Place bed rails back in place.

"Mrs. Jones, would you like your light left on or off?"

"I have plenty of time to help you with anything that you need to help make your time in the hospital as comfortable as possible, so is there anything else I can do for you?"

8. Thank the patient.

If there is nothing else you can do, hand the patient a tent card and continue, "Here is a card that has my name and my director's name and my director's phone number printed on it. Should you have any problems or if there is anything we can do for you, please do not hesitate to call. Thank you, Mrs. Jones."

ENCOUNTERING RESISTANCE

Not everyone in your organization will readily embrace the idea of scripting. Some employees may feel that they're being asked to say things that are unnatural. Others just may not want to be limited to a certain set of words and behaviors. Over time, however, we have found that these vocal opponents of scripting will likely become its strongest proponents.

Leaders can do their part to encourage these resistors by rewarding employees who use scripting, developing games and exercises to help all employees become more comfortable with the practice, and consciously reinforcing the value of scripting at every opportunity. In some cases, however, it may just take time.

One of our nurse leaders tells an amusing story about her attitude transformation regarding scripts:

Lynn Pierce, a lead nurse consultant with our Baptist Leadership Institute and former nursing leader of Baptist Hospital's 45-bed medical telemetry unit, was quite skeptical in the early days of our cultural transformation. When we implemented scripting, emphasizing the difference it could make in achieving consistently high levels of patient satisfaction, Lynn quietly made a pact with another nurse leader that they would not cooperate. She simply did not want to be told what to say! Lynn recalls that she would read the newly developed scripts and make jokes about them to other employees.

The patient satisfaction scores for the medical telemetry unit were actually some of the lowest in the hospital. Lynn thought that if she quietly went about her business that her colleagues would not notice that she was having trouble "buying in" to the transition to a customer-focused culture. While other nurses who reported to her were already seeing the value of scripting, Lynn stubbornly resisted.

One day, while making her nursing rounds, Lynn encountered a patient that she still refers to as "one of the meanest men in the world." As she started to introduce herself the patient interrupted her, harshly asking, "Are you my nurse? What do you want?" Caught off guard by his reaction, Lynn acknowledges that she didn't know how to respond. She wanted to reply, "I don't want anything! I really don't want to be here, and I don't want to encounter rude and unappreciative patients on my rounds." But she was aware that the CEO had just handed out letters that actually asked patients to call him anytime he could be of help to them. He had even listed his office *and* his home phone number. So instead of reacting by saying something negative, she remembered all those scripts that she had previously joked about.

Lynn started by calmly introducing herself as the nurse leader and explaining that she would like to take care of any needs that the patient had. She then continued using other scripted messages, letting the patient know of a variety of ways to contact her and assuring him she had the time to attend to his needs during his hospital stay. She proceeded to use every scripted message she could remember. By the end of the encounter, she had won the patient over. He even went out of his way to comment about how nice she was. A little ashamed, she thought to herself, "If you only knew . . . "

It took this dramatic incident for Lynn to realize that the tools and practices we had initiated really did work. When she shared her experience with the nurse manager with whom she had made the pact, her colleague confessed that she had been using scripting for a month, and that it had already accounted for an increase in patient satisfaction scores for her unit.

Today, Lynn is one of our biggest supporters of scripting because she has personally experienced its effectiveness. She can sympathize with new nurses who hesitate to use scripts, and she can share the story of her own attitude adjustment.

SCRIPT FOR CONSISTENT SUCCESS

Imagine every individual in your organization using words and gestures that are in perfect harmony with your mission, vision, and values. This is the power that scripting has, and it is not lost on customers. Several years ago, the wife of one of our physicians was hospitalized at Baptist, and I went by to visit with her. Both she and her husband had been involved at another local hospital before they joined our team. As soon as I walked into her room, she said, "Al, there really is a difference."

I said, "Tell me what you are talking about."

She said, "Even the housekeeper stopped as she was leaving and asked, 'Is there anything else I can do for you? I have the time.' She cared enough to stop and ask that question. Wow!"

Effective scripting benefits everyone. Customers benefit by hearing a consistent message from the time they arrive until the time they leave. Employees benefit by being empowered to offer world-class service while communicating utmost care and concern for their customers. As you make the commitment to service excellence in your organization, I urge you to take advantage of this powerful tool.

CHAPTER 11

Developing Rounding and Service Recovery Techniques

I like to ask top executives this question: What percentage of your employees could pick you out of a police line-up?

—Brian Jones, Baptist Leadership
Institute Consultant

When I speak to different groups around the country about our transformation, I often use a "from this to that" model to describe the changes that our WOW! culture has required of our leaders. For instance, we had to move from a financial focus to a balanced focus, as I described in my discussion of our five pillars, and from a telling mindset to an asking mindset, which we have done with tools like Bright Ideas and other communication forums.

Another vital "from this to that" transition that our leadership team had to make was "from invisible to visible." We had to make sure that our employees knew who we were and felt confident and comfortable approaching us. I, along with the rest of our management team, had to learn to get out of my office and become an open-minded, open-door, open-book people person. This was crucial to creating the "open communication, no secrets" culture that our employees desired.

Before 1995, I could easily go a week or more without ever leaving the administrative suite during the workday. "After all," I reasoned, "I have a lot of important stuff to do!"

In our new culture, that mindset was no longer an option. A true commitment to open communication meant that we had to spend time becoming engaged with our workforce. We just had to get out there and do it. When the members of our management team caught the spirit of getting out of the office, our employees took notice and responded to our increased visibility and accessibility. We learned to enjoy making rounds and being available to our employees, physicians, and patients, and we saw quick and impressive results. Visibility boosted credibility.

WHAT IS ROUNDING?

What I have described above is the practice of senior leader rounding—one of the three main types of rounding that we practice. The others are department leader and nurse leader rounding. We expect all of our leaders to make rounding a regular part of their day, but the leader's goals differ at different levels of the organization. Let me briefly describe each type of rounding that we practice:

Nurse Leader Rounding

A nurse leader's primary objective in rounding is to see patients and their families in their rooms to ensure that the highest quality care is being provided during each shift. They visit each patient in their unit, recognizing that their direct contact with patients and their families enables them as nurses to evaluate the quality of our service from the customer's perspective. Giving our customers numerous opportunities to share any concerns or needs with us enables us to do all we can to guarantee optimal patient satisfaction.

A rounding nurse leader asks each patient specific questions to assess the care they have received. "Have the nurses come when your call light was pushed?" "Have you gotten your medications on time?" "Is there anything we can do to make you more comfortable?" They check things like IVs and telemetry equipment to ensure that our clinical quality remains high. If they do identify a problem, they are able to correct it immediately and make the proper staff member aware of it.

Nurse leaders also talk with patients and family members to discover concerns about the care they have received or simply to identify opportunities for improvement. As they visit each room, they quickly scan to identify needs; for example, if a light bulb is out, the nurse leader makes the call right then, from the patient's room, to ask for its replacement. In our pretransformation days, our patient satisfaction surveys were batched and looked at every month or so by the administrative team (if we got around to it), making it next to impossible for us to discover that a patient's television remote didn't work or that there were not enough blankets to make him or her comfortable before that patient had left our care. Rounding enables our nurse leaders to take immediate action when they discover a need and also to initiate service recovery procedures with a patient when necessary. I will share more about our service recovery procedures later in this chapter.

Department Leader Rounding

Department leaders spend most of their rounding time in their own department. These leaders round for four main reasons: First, to monitor quality. Just as with nurse leaders, rounding enables department leaders to assess the levels of service that our staff is providing and make corrections or adjustment as necessary. Second, rounding gives leaders a chance to reward and recognize team members. When a leader sees an employee living out our values, exceeding our standards of performance, or going the extra mile to provide superior service to a customer, he can offer timely and relevant praise for that employee's efforts.

The third reason department leaders round is to teach and train employees. When employees know that their leaders are eager and willing to help them, they will not hesitate to ask for instruction or assistance when they need it. Rounding enables leaders to identify training needs and either meet the need right then or develop a plan to see that it is met as quickly as possible. The fourth reason to round is that it provides a chance for service recovery. When a service failure is discovered, leaders can see that the recovery process is implemented and can follow up on the results (see Figure 11.1).

Senior Leader Rounding

Our senior leaders spend time rounding everywhere in the organization. They make it their objective to see and interact with every department. When employees see their senior leaders spending significant time in locations throughout the organization, they become comfortable with the members of their management team. Visibility of the senior leadership

FIGURE 11.1 Reasons for Department Leader Rounding

- Monitor quality
- Reward and Recognize Team Members
- Teach and Train Employees
- Provides a Chance for Service Recovery

team enhances leader-employee relationships and creates a sense of equal value in all departments. When this happens, employees become more fully engaged and more likely to share with us what is really on their minds.

As senior leaders, we round to get a "big picture" feel for the organization. After I have spent time in a certain department, no matter what the department, I have a clearer understanding of the needs of those employees and patients and a better picture of how my actions affect their service and satisfaction. I know what tools, programs, and support those employees need to do their jobs effectively. Seeing their work firsthand gives me a valuable new perspective.

We also round to build relationships with employees. Consistency and familiarity are keys to building any relationship, and they are necessary for creating a WOW! environment. One visit to a department won't do much for building a relationship, but when an employee learns that he can expect to see my face weekly—or even daily—in his department, he knows that I am serious about being involved and building a relationship. I can then expect those employees to provide valuable feedback and to share with me when they have a need or identify an opportunity for improvement.

Like department leaders, senior leaders can also use rounding time to reward and recognize outstanding employees. If a department has achieved a record level of patient satisfaction, I need to know about it so that I can recognize that accomplishment. I may observe a behavior while I am rounding that deserves a personal thank-you note, or I may hear from employees about a department head or manager who needs to be rewarded. Rounding enables all of our management team to offer praise and recognition for things we would never know about if we remained sequestered in our offices.

As president of Baptist Hospital, John Heer diligently protected his rounding time each day because he was convinced of its importance. "It's important to demonstrate to staff that you support their efforts and that their feedback will be used to make the organization better. Rounding is a great tool to reward and acknowledge your staff's performance or discover areas for improvement. This is your time to engage staff and find out what they need. Rounding is not a program—it is a *best practice* to impact the culture of the organization and create positive results."

ROUNDING PREPARATION

Our leaders must spend some time preparing in order to get the most out of their rounding time. The first step is to determine the best time to round. This will vary from department to department, and the best way to find out is to simply ask. Members of a department will quickly be able to tell you when your visit will be most effective. Our senior leaders have found that they should avoid early morning and shift changes, when staff members are busy performing assessments, talking with physicians and giving medications; rounding at other times will allow them time to communicate with nurses and physicians, which is their primary objective. Our nurse leaders, however, have found that early morning is the best time to make rounds to patients' rooms; they can observe the nightshift's work, inspect the status of patients' rooms, check IV fluids, and see if medications were left at the bedside. Each department will have its own best time to round based on the functions that its team members perform, and leaders can make the most of their rounding time by visiting during prime hours.

Before our leaders round, we ask them to do their homework. Each leader must determine exactly what he or she wants to accomplish by rounding. We encourage our leaders to make a mental or written list of their objectives and to think about how they will observe and communicate, recognizing that their attitude and countenance will greatly influence the effectiveness of their rounding. Purposes for rounding will vary; some visits may be to communicate a certain message, while others may be mostly to glean information and suggestions from employees. Leaders must know their purpose to have a successful rounding experience.

Doing their homework also means learning about the department or patients they will be visiting. As senior leaders, we need to learn as much as we can about a department before we round, including the names of employees, the jobs that department team members perform, and that department's most recent survey results or other noteworthy accomplishments. I may

FIGURE 11.2 Rounding Preparation

- Get your attitude together.
- Know your purpose.
- Have knowledge of the department or unit and the staff.
- Check the best time to round with the department.
- Start where you're most comfortable.
- Have a pad and pen ready to take notes.
- Have business cards available to distribute.
- Know the patient satisfaction scores in that area.

even call or e-mail a department head to get the names of certain employees who deserve recognition. The more I know about a department ahead of time, the more I can connect with and relate to the employees that I encounter on my rounds.

Sharing facts about a department with that department's employees while rounding can be effective for senior and department leaders. For example, in a medical unit, we may want to share how much a semiprivate room costs per night to encourage employees to provide the best service to those who pay their salaries—the patients. In a plant operations department, knowing how many service calls workers have completed that week enables us to thank them specifically for the work they do to keep the facility running smoothly. Discovering these kinds of facts doesn't take long, but it speaks volumes to employees about the value they have to the organization (see Figure 11.2).

ROUNDING SCRIPTS

One final step in rounding preparation is to develop a script. As I explained in Chapter 10, Scripting for Superior Service, scripting enables leaders to determine the best way to convey the message they want to send. By carefully choosing our words and actions, we ensure that our message will be consistent with our culture and values.

A department or senior leader might use a script similar to this one to "break the ice" and get the communication flowing:

> I'm _____, the (title) of (organization or department). I wanted to say hello and make sure that your needs are being met.
>
> Is there anything I can do to make it easier for you to do your job? (Ask follow-up questions about any suggestions the employee has.)
>
> I'd like to hear about any ideas you may have to help make our organization better. (Again, ask follow-up questions and, if necessary, develop a plan of action.)

My experience has been that once employees see that you are serious about interacting with them and gaining their feedback, they will gladly offer their opinions and suggestions. By your third or fourth visit to a department, you may not get to say a word before employees start sharing their stories and ideas. Until they are comfortable with you, however, using a script can help to neutralize any tension they may feel about having a leader in their area and enable you to communicate most effectively.

As with all of our scripts for patient-employee interactions, our nurse leader scripts have been carefully designed to convey the message that we want to send to our patients. Here is a script that a nurse leader might use while making rounds:

> I'm _____, the (title) of (department or unit). I wanted to say hello and make sure your needs are being met. We're sorry that you're sick, but we would like to thank you for allowing us the opportunity to take care of your health needs. We want to exceed your expectations. If there is anything I can help you with, here is my number. Please don't hesitate to let me know.

Nurse, department, and senior leaders will want to identify key questions to ask while they are rounding. They may even want to write out a checklist. For example, nurses would want to be sure to ask patients about the quality of care, the cleanliness of the room, the timeliness of call light responses, and the friendliness of staff. Department and senior leaders would want to ask employees about the adequacy of staffing and supplies, special needs in the department, and any barriers staff have encountered to providing great service. Having appropriate questions ready will show that you are truly concerned about your patients and employees and will enable you to make valuable discoveries during your rounding time.

PROBLEM SOLVING WHILE ROUNDING

Leaders who round will occasionally encounter problems. In fact, one of the reasons you are rounding is to find problems and fix them before they become major issues. Because nurse leaders are rounding with patients, their problem solving falls under the heading of service recovery, which I will discuss later. Senior leaders and department leaders, however, must address employee problems, and the manner in which they do this can greatly affect morale and employee satisfaction.

Colin Powell once said, "The day people stop bringing you their problems is the day you stop leading them." As leaders, we should be glad when employees feel comfortable bringing us their concerns and frustrations. They are giving us the chance to improve their work situation rather than saying nothing and letting the problem grow. How we respond when an employee tells us about a problem will communicate either care and empowerment or apathy and lack of concern.

Our senior leaders have found that the most effective way to handle an employee's problem is to engage that employee in the problem solving process. By asking staff to participate in finding a solution, we demonstrate confidence in their capabilities and tap into our employees' knowledge of their department and situation, which is almost always greater than our own. The sooner we address the concern the better, so we typically brainstorm right then with the employee about how to solve the problem. While some problems may be too complex to solve in a five-minute brainstorming session, many times this is all it takes. When we have determined a workable solution, we decide who needs to take action and get to work.

The final component in this problem-solving process is to follow up. A quick e-mail sent when I get back to my office can inform a manager of the problem we addressed and the solution we created. A handwritten thank-you note can acknowledge an employee's successful problem solving and encourage him or her to continue to find better ways to do things. Following up gives me the chance to express appreciation for the hard work our employees are doing, and it lets them know that I haven't forgotten about their situation just because I have left their department. It is a final step that is easy to skip, but it will prove itself worth the time it takes in employee satisfaction. When leaders tell me that they would love to round but don't have time, I tell them that they don't have time not to round. And the busier, more hectic their day is, or the greater and more complex the problems are, the more they should be rounding.

SERVICE RECOVERY

When nurse leaders round, they see patients instead of staff, and therefore encounter different types of problems. When our nurse leaders or other employees discover a problem of any kind with the care we are providing, it is time to initiate service recovery.

We understand and acknowledge that we will occasionally drop the ball and disappoint a customer. As wonderful as they are, our employees are not perfect, and they will make mistakes. What we have found, however, is that how we respond when we make a mistake can mean the difference between a dissatisfied customer and a fanatically loyal customer. Small drops in our service level are not guarantees of decreased satisfaction if we handle these situations correctly.

Before we can begin to practice service recovery, we must become aware of a problem. In our pretransformation culture, our patient feedback systems were so slow that we often didn't learn of service failures until a patient had been out of our care for weeks or months. Today, we give patients as many opportunities as we can to let us know immediately if anything is not up to their expectations. As I mentioned above, nurse leader rounding is a valuable tool for discovering service issues that need to be addressed. By visiting every patient every day and asking the right questions on those visits, our nurse leaders ensure that patients have the opportunity to voice any concerns or complaints that they have.

Another practice we have implemented is the delivery of a welcome letter to every new patient on his or her first day in the hospital. This letter, signed by the hospital administrator, welcomes patients and thanks them for choosing us to meet their health needs. Then it goes on to say, "If you want to discuss your care, please let a staff member know your thoughts, or call me here or at home" (see Figure 11.3). How many hospital administrators (or business leaders of any kind) give out their home phone number to all of their customers? We do it because we are serious about receiving customer feedback, and because we want to know when we need to initiate service recovery. Now, does the administrator get deluged

FIGURE 11.3 Patient Letter from Administrator

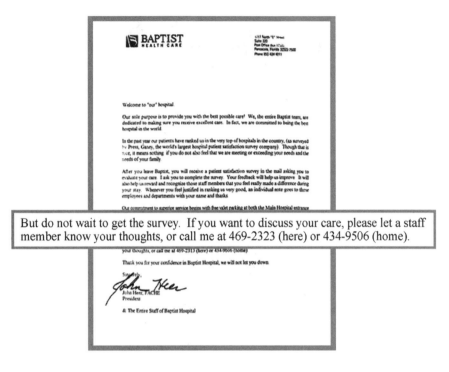

at home with phone calls? No. Does he get one every six months? Yes. Is he glad he got that one so that he can take some steps toward ser-vice recovery? Absolutely.

ACT FOR SERVICE RECOVERY

Once we have become aware of a problem, we want to get busy correcting it. This is where many organizations get into trouble. Far too many hospitals and healthcare workers believe that it is enough to simply fix the patient's problem. If all we do is simply address the concern without making up for a patient's inconvenience or discomfort, that patient has still had a negative experience. For this reason, we teach our employees to go one step further, not only fixing the problem but also doing something extra to make amends.

Our employees follow a three-step process, represented in the acronym

ACT, to handle all service recoveries. The first step is to **Apologize** for the service failure. Because this is such a crucial time in determining customer satisfaction, we have created scripts for our employees to use in various service recovery situations. The employee usually begins the apology by stating, "That is not the way we like for things to be here at _____. We clearly did not meet your expectations." This is not the time to make excuses for the mistake or blame coworkers or other departments. We simply want to acknowledge that a mistake was made and that we are sorry for it.

The second step is to **Correct** the problem, on the spot if possible. The service failure must be addressed immediately, but as I said earlier, this is not enough to create a loyal, satisfied customer. Therefore, we empower all of our employees to not just correct, but to "Correct PLUS." If a patient has had a negative experience of any kind, we need to do something special to overshadow the bad experience with a good one.

Bob Murphy uses the following illustration when he describes our service recovery procedures to new employees: "If I visit a restaurant, have my order messed up, and get nothing for it except a corrected order fifteen minutes after everyone else has eaten, I will not leave with positive feelings about that restaurant. If, however, the waiter corrects my order, apologizes for the inconvenience, doesn't charge me for my meal, *and* offers us a free dessert, I'll be talking about it for a week. I'll tell my friends about the excellent service we received, and I'll be coming back to eat there again soon." That's what we mean by "Correct PLUS."

We have created numerous channels to perform service recovery. Each of our employees is authorized to offer patients free meal tickets to the cafeteria or service apology gift certificates for the hospital gift shop. All of our employees can spend up to $20 in the hospital gift shop any time it's open to do service recovery, and we encourage them to use this option. If a patient is upset with the cleanliness of her room, we want our employees to first see that the room is adequately cleaned, but then to also deliver a small bouquet of flowers from the gift shop to help "brighten things up." We want to exceed our patients' expectations, especially after a service failure.

I sometimes see mouths drop open when I tell groups that we give every employee the authority to spend up to $250 to do service recovery. Whether they need to replace a lost item, offer a service apology gift check for the gift shop or the cafe (see Figure 11.4), or choose an item from the gift shop to help make amends, our employees are empowered to take immediate action to solve the problem and exceed patient expectations. In addition, they are inspired with the knowledge that management trusts them not to abuse this privilege. Motivated employees and loyal customers are worth the expense of service recovery, which is lower than you might think.

Last year, our largest hospital, Baptist Hospital, spent about $8,000 on service recovery. Considering the customer loyalty that we gain through these practices, we don't believe that we can afford *not* to do it. I would gladly spend much more than $8,000 to make sure that my customers will come back, and while we can't guarantee this for every patient, our experience has shown that effective service recovery is one of the best things we can do to create radically loyal customers. Your service recovery efforts will pay for themselves many times over in repeat customers, word-of-mouth advertising, and increased customer satisfaction. In addition to those benefits, the positive message that we send to our workforce that we trust them not to abuse this privilege is almost immeasurable.

Nurse leader Lynn Pierce tells of a time when service recovery made the difference between an angry patient and a loyal customer. A visually-impaired man in his sixties was fighting a very high temperature, and his doctor decided to admit him to Baptist Hospital. He arrived at the admissions department just as they were closing for the day, so they sent him to the Emergency Room to be admitted. When his wife, who had dropped him off at admissions, finally found him in the ER, she waited with him over an hour before he could be admitted because the ER did not have his paperwork.

To make matters worse, the nurse who was responsible for administering

FIGURE 11.4 Apology Gift Certificate

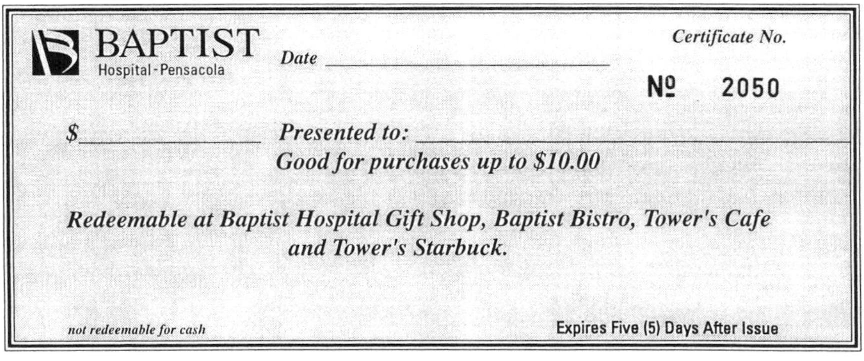
BAPTIST
Hospital-Pensacola

Date ____________________

Certificate No.

№ 2050

$ ____________ *Presented to:* ____________________

Good for purchases up to $10.00

Redeemable at Baptist Hospital Gift Shop, Baptist Bistro, Tower's Cafe and Tower's Starbuck.

not redeemable for cash

Expires Five (5) Days After Issue

the medication to bring down his fever was distracted during her shift change and forgot to deliver it. The couple waited over two hours before anything was done about this man's temperature, which was the reason he had been admitted. By this point, they were understandably upset. The man had always used another local hospital before that day, and he expressed his disgust with the service he had received at Baptist.

Thankfully, his nurses took action to see that service recovery was performed. Because of the couple's wait in the ER, the nurses asked a leader from that department to visit the couple and apologize for the inconvenience, which he did. They also moved the patient to a private room so that his wife could stay with him around the clock. Then, in visiting with the patient, the nurses made an interesting discovery. The couple was getting ready to celebrate their first anniversary. The man was not only unhappy with our service, but he was upset about being admitted to the hospital in the first place because he had already made plans to go shopping for his wife's anniversary present.

FIGURE 11.5 Service Recovery Database

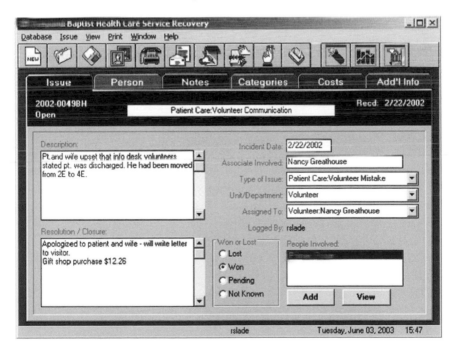

Our staff decided that this couple would get to celebrate their anniversary, even if they were stuck in the hospital. An employee called catering and asked them to prepare a nice meal, complete with "fancy folded napkins," for the couple to share. They gave the man a small, crystal ornament from the gift shop to give his wife, and did everything else they could think of to ensure that they had a special—and memorable—first anniversary.

How do you think this man feels about Baptist Hospital today? I assure you, customers don't get any more loyal than he is! With effective service recovery, we were able to turn a terrible experience into a positive memory that this couple will share for the rest of their lives.

The final step our employees follow in service recovery is to **Trend** the results so that we can learn from our mistakes. We carefully track every service failure, recording the date and description of the incident, department or unit involved, person responsible, and recovery actions taken (including the amount spent). This information is reported via a special extension to an operator who records it and sees that it is entered into a service recovery database (pictured in Figure 11.5). Keeping track of service failures in this manner helps us to recognize trends, analyze causes, and develop and implement solutions for avoiding future failures. We see every service failure as an opportunity for improvement, and we want to see that the same mistake does not happen twice. Trending holds employees accountable for improving their service and constantly raising the level of care that they provide, reflecting our ongoing commitment to service excellence in every facet of our organization.

KEY FOUR

CONTINUOUSLY DEVELOP GREAT LEADERS

Effective leaders are critical to your success. According to Marcus Buckingham and Curt Coffman, authors of *First Break All the Rules* (Simon & Schuster, 1999), "Talented employees need great managers. The talented employee may join a company because of its charismatic leaders, its generous benefits, and its world-class training programs, but how long that employee stays and how productive he is while he is there is determined by his relationship with his immediate supervisor." Gallup studies have shown that as many as sixty percent of employees who leave an organization do so because they don't like or can't get along with their direct supervisor. As we continued our journey toward becoming a WOW! organization, we became convinced that without trained, effective leaders at every level, we would never be able to sustain the success we were achieving.

In Chapter 12, Establishing Ongoing Leadership Training, I want to recount the development of our leadership training programs. We have gone from offering very little formal leadership training of any kind to gaining national recognition as people developers. In 2004, for the second year in a row, our leadership development program, anchored by Baptist University, was included in *Training* Magazine's Top 100 Training Programs in America and listed as one of the "global elite." Also as a result of our leadership development efforts, I was recognized as one of eleven "CEOs Who Get It" in *Training's* 2002 "Movers and Shakers" issue. Their short list of CEOs who have made people development a priority put me in the company of the CEOs of Pfizer, Best Buy, and Dow Chemical.

How did that happen? It happened because of an early recognition that to be successful, we needed to make a consistent, ongoing investment in developing leaders at every level of our organization. I hope you can learn from our experience and make your organization one that actively invests in its leaders.

CHAPTER 12

Establishing Ongoing Leadership Training

If you stop learning today, you stop leading tomorrow.
—Howard Hendricks,
author and speaker

Too often in health care, the only difference between the best floor nurse in a department and head nurse for that department is seventy-two hours over the weekend to decide if she really wants the job. While this nurse may have been wonderfully competent in her previous role, a promotion to head nurse makes her suddenly responsible for hiring and firing, supervising, motivating, disciplining, scheduling, and overseeing patient care. What tools have we given her to help her grow from being a great nurse to a great nurse leader? How have we prepared her for her new role? If we aren't careful, not only have we failed this new leader, but we have also lost our best floor nurse!

A strong leadership development program meets this need. In order to reach our goals of service excellence and unparalleled patient satisfaction, we know that we need motivated, satisfied employees; they are the ones who will provide the quality care that drives service excellence. We also know that employees will be most satisfied when their leaders maintain a high standard of leadership excellence and that to achieve this leadership excellence, our leaders need continuous development of leadership skills. Putting programs in place to develop leaders contributes to employee satisfaction in two

159

ways: Our leaders (who are also employees) become more satisfied because we are constantly teaching them to do their jobs better, and those who they are leading become more satisfied because their department heads and managers are becoming better leaders. These satisfied, trained employees are then better equipped to provide the high level of customer service that we expect. Employees are happier and patients are happier, and that makes management happy, too.

We have not attained our status as a nationally recognized people developer without investing significant time and effort, nor would this achievement have been possible without an unwavering commitment from the people who have made it happen. As I share the steps we took to establish our leadership development programs—and how they are evolving to this day—I hope you will take the lessons we have learned and use them to begin developing your people. Bottom line: There is no better way to improve employee satisfaction (which drives patient satisfaction) than to improve the quality of the leadership and supervision employees receive.

STEP 1: DEFINE THE GAP

In the years leading up to our cultural change, Baptist Health Care had grown quite rapidly. Two hospitals in south Alabama joined our corporation in 1995, and we added a behavioral medicine facility in 1996. While we may have been one unified system on paper, in reality the members of the leadership team that resulted from these mergers barely knew each other's names. Each company had its own mission statement, operating procedures, and cultural identity. We were not culturally unified, and quite honestly, the various entities were not even sure they wanted to be unified. We had a long way to go to achieve the excellence we desired, and we recognized that we would need strong leaders to take us there.

As we embarked on our journey toward transformation, we began with an honest look at where we were. In early 1996, our employee morale was frighteningly low. Our most recent employee attitude survey had identified a need for improvement in almost every area. We knew that senior management was not going to be able to drive our transformation without support from the rest of our leaders. We could go only so far on emotion. It was time to build some leadership "muscle" among our middle managers.

We knew that strong leadership was a necessary element in our new culture, but we didn't yet have the tools in place to develop those leaders.

Working with Sperduto and Associates, the Atlanta-based firm that performed our employee attitude survey, a group of senior leaders performed a gap analysis of our leadership development program. We asked, and answered, three questions: (1) Where are we now regarding leadership development? (2) Where do we want to be in five years? ten years? (3) What will it take to get there?

This evaluation exercise led us to identify our substantial need for a reformed and expanded leadership development program, and it challenged us to dream about the kind of people developers we hoped to become. We decided to start with a focus on developing our middle managers, which would encompass approximately 300 leaders across our organization. Once we had clearly defined this target, we were able to quickly mobilize the right people to begin achieving our leadership development goals. That leads me to Step 2.

STEP 2: ORGANIZE YOUR EFFORTS

As we did in so many other areas, we wanted to make this leadership emphasis an employee driven approach, so we decided to create a leadership development program that would be run by a steering committee of middle managers with guidance from a senior leader. The next question was how to select the middle managers who would take this new initiative and put it into action. We knew we would be asking them to accept responsibilities on top of their regular work load, and we needed to make sure that they were up to the challenge.

To identify the right people for the job, we asked the following question of every leader in our organization: "If you were going to Mars to build a brand new society and you could only take with you five leaders from our organization, who would they be?" When the results were tabulated, we had a short list of people whose names had shown up repeatedly. We asked those leaders—who had already gained the trust, respect, and admiration of their peers—to become the steering committee for our new leadership development program. As effective leaders themselves, they were glad to be a part of our new effort.

We wanted to ensure that our new program had the right emphasis, so we set out to identify the most important concepts and principles to teach as well as the methods we would use to teach them. Several members of the senior management team worked with the steering committee to establish some guiding principles for the new program. We used our mission, vision, and values and considered the most pressing needs of our organization to develop guidelines for the committee to use as they took us through this process. We settled on seven principles for the steering committee to follow:

1. Individual growth and development will be a fundamental emphasis and will be included in each session. We will seek to promote personal growth by encouraging leaders to perform self-assessment exercises, conduct 360-degree feedback surveys, create a developmental plan, keep a journal of insights and thoughts during the year, write a personal value statement and management philosophy, and the like.

When we asked employees to describe the qualities of great leaders they have known, less than one-half of one percent of the qualities they listed relate to technical skills. When I share this with our leaders, I also challenge them, "How much of your time are you spending developing technical skills versus developing leadership skills? If most of your time is spent on the technical aspect of your job, then you are, in a sense, perfectly misaligned."

2. Emphasis will also be on team play, networking, and building relationships. We will look for every opportunity to allow individuals to develop a connection with as many other individuals as possible, thus creating a web of relationships across institutions, departments, and so on. To begin with, we will assign individuals to small learning teams that will remain intact across the year. We will also look for opportunities to emphasize the value and importance of diversity; each team's makeup will maximize diversity across levels, facilities, division, gender, race, and so on.

3. Involvement of senior management is key. We will involve at least one senior manager in a presentation/facilitation/leadership role during each session, and all will be present at the kick off session.

4. Much recognition, reward, and celebration will be included. We want this to be a fun, exciting, motivating process.

5. Participants will be heavily involved in planning and executing the process. We will ensure this through the use of the steering committee and a subcommittee structure. We will also encourage peer consultation within the learning teams, the sharing of best practices, and the use of participants with special areas of expertise as presenters.

One of the questions I am frequently asked is, "Why do you let people get away from their job responsibilities to serve on these leadership development teams? Doesn't that hurt the organization?" When answering this, I always relate the story of Clif Colley, our Director of Decision Support in Finance, and leader of one of our key leadership development teams. Clif had gotten very involved in his work in leadership development, and I asked his boss, Eleanor McGee, Vice President of Finance, if his work was suffering because of this time commitment. She said, "No way! In fact, working on leadership development has given Clif so much confidence and knowledge that right now he is a better Director of Decision Support than he has ever been." Invest in your leaders' development—you will never regret it.

6. There will be an emphasis on contributing back to the organization. We will focus on providing practical skills and user-friendly tools so that the participants can make immediate use of what they are learning.

7. We will use a variety of training processes to keep people interested and motivated. These processes include individual activities, small and large group work, self-study, learning team homework assignments, reading materials, case studies, videos, outside presenters, internal presenters, and panel discussions. We will also maximize the amount of information and number of ideas we provide individuals ("load their minds" to get their creative juices flowing).

KICKING THINGS OFF

We held a kick off luncheon for senior leaders and the sixteen members of the steering committee, where we briefly looked at where we were and then focused on where we wanted to go. I challenged the committee to believe that a leadership development program could help us achieve the cultural change that we desired. We looked together at the guiding principles that we had established and discussed the structure of the steering committee. Then I asked each individual to personally commit to making our new program successful. Every member agreed.

We scheduled seven two-day training sessions over the next eighteen months for our 300 middle managers, with the first session to be held just seven weeks after the kick off meeting. We knew that the sooner we started training our leaders, the stronger our organization would become, and we also felt that the sense of urgency created by a close deadline would be a good motivator for this new team. As you establish your own leadership development program, I encourage you to set a tight time table for your team; the sooner you begin investing in your leaders, the sooner they can begin applying the lessons they've learned, and the sooner you will begin seeing results.

Our team rose to the challenge beautifully, quickly forming six sub-committees—Curriculum, Logistics, Social, Celebrations, Communications, and Diversity—to prepare for the first session. Members of the steering committee served as chair and cochair on each subcommittee, and they were responsible for recruiting team members to complete their committee. Again, I want to emphasize that all of these committee members accepted these responsibilities in addition to their regular workload. Only one member of our steering committee had leadership development as her only job description—our Director of People Development. All of the others were regular employees who believed so strongly in the value of leadership development that they were willing to devote the extra time and energy necessary to make it happen.

This was our initial organizational structure. In the eight years that we have been focusing on developing our leaders, we have made some significant changes to our programs, and I will share some of those later in this chapter. As we began our journey, however, this committee structure and set of guiding principles proved to be valuable tools in establishing an effective program.

STEP 3: DEVELOP AND IMPLEMENT

The steering committee quickly got to work preparing for their first session. Their first objective was to create an identity for the new program, so they began discussing possible names and ideas. After a good deal of brainstorming they chose the name *Bridges*, meant to symbolize both a bridge connecting all of the Baptist Health Care entities and a bridge into the twenty-first century, which was fast approaching. They developed a bridge logo (see Figure 12.1) and even asked our maintenance department to build a real-life bridge that they could assemble for each session. The construction of the bridge at our first session was a symbolic and inspiring time as each officer and administrator added a piece of the bridge to complete its

FIGURE 12.1 Bridges Logo

assembly. Creating an identity for your leadership program will serve to unite the steering team and create a sense of ownership as well as fostering interest throughout the organization.

To communicate the purpose of our new venture, the steering committee also created a vision statement:

> Building the country's best leaders for the country's best health care system

and a mission statement:

> To develop leaders within Baptist Health Care who create and promote a culture of excellence

They then turned their attention to the content of the leadership training sessions. In order to identify the most pressing curriculum needs, they asked our middle managers to participate in a leader's needs assessment in which they indicated which areas they would most like the Bridges sessions to address from a list of possible topics including communication, stress management, delegation, negotiation, team building, and other leadership issues. By asking our leaders where they wanted help, the steering committee was able to target a large number of leaders with each session and create curriculum that would be eagerly embraced by our "students."

With the knowledge of our leaders' needs, the steering committee next created a comprehensive list of "deliverables." In this list they sought to identify all of the areas in which our leaders needed high competency in order to promote and sustain our WOW! culture. The list of deliverables coupled with the results of the leader's needs assessments became their roadmap for creating the seven Bridges sessions. They decided on the topics that each session would cover and the celebrations committee developed a clever theme to fit the topic. For session 2, "Refining Your Personal Skills," they chose the theme "Mirror, Mirror, On the Wall," and for the session entitled "Mining Your Resources," they used a pirate theme to encourage leaders to "dig up the treasure" in their departments. The curriculum committee selected speakers, chose reading materials, and set the course agenda, while the logistics committee took care of the details for the day—parking, food, rosters, registration, and so on. Each of the committees worked tirelessly to make our seven Bridges sessions a success.

The program kicked off in February 1997, and we enjoyed an immediate positive response from our participants. Three significant results came from those eighteen months of Bridges sessions. First, we made great strides in bringing the varied parts of our health system together into one family. Our very first session included a showcase of each Baptist Health Care entity, and our leaders began to gain a broader perspective of the organization. They began communicating with each other, sharing ideas and best practices, and all of our entities benefited from it. Second, we began to experience the advantages of sharing a common language across the breadth of the organization. In the Bridges sessions, our 300 middle managers became familiar with terms that would be integral to our new culture, such as our five pillars, accountability tools, and core values. We could then use these terms freely in our communication with staff and trust that they would be understood. The third significant outcome from the Bridges sessions was that we identified a creative, committed group of employees who enjoyed piloting our leadership development efforts—and did it well. As we neared the end of that eighteen months, it became clear that we were just beginning the leadership development journey, and we began to consider our options for continuing and expanding the people developing arm of our organization.

STEP 4: ADJUST AND EVOLVE

We were pleased with the success of the Bridges program, but we also recognized that we could not simply rest on what we had already accomplished. In order to keep up with the needs of our employees—and to reach our goals for employee and patient satisfaction—we needed to expand our education efforts even further.

We knew that we wanted to put in place a permanent leadership development structure. We also recognized that for that structure to be successful it needed to have unequivocal support from the officers and administrators throughout the organization. The reality was that while many of those top leaders had actively participated in the Bridges effort, some sat on the sidelines. We took our group of senior leaders and formed *Baptist University for Learning and Leading* (BULL).

That mechanism became an ongoing leadership development tool for our senior leadership team that is still in place to this day. Our twenty-eight senior leaders meet for a half-day every quarter to accomplish two primary purposes. Our first goal is pure leadership development, stemming from a recognition that even the team that has "made it to the top" still needs to be growing and developing as leaders. The second purpose of the session is to provide direction and ownership to our larger leadership development initiatives across the organization.

As our senior leaders considered our employees' continued needs for leadership education, we determined that the end of Bridges could not mean the end of our education efforts. In response to the need for ongoing leadership education for our employees, we created *Baptist University* (BU), a formalized ongoing education initiative for our Baptist Health Care leaders. I asked Pam Bilbrey, our senior vice president for corporate services and clearly one of the most gifted people developers I have worked with in my thirty-year career, to be the initial chairperson of BU. She still serves in that role today.

We made several changes to Baptist University as compared to its predecessor, the Bridges program. One change was to require anyone who was a supervisor of any kind to participate in BU sessions; this grew our "class size" from 300 to almost 600 Baptist Health Care leaders, allowing us to expand the influence of our education efforts. We told these 600 leaders to expect to invest a full day, once a quarter, in an off-campus Baptist University training session where they would be equipped as leaders and as healthcare workers.

As we excitedly anticipated the expansion of Baptist University, we felt the need to clearly determine our objectives. We asked ourselves, "If we're going to continue to pour our resources into developing our leaders, what is the skill set that we want them to develop? What does a well-developed leader look like?" The answer to these questions would serve as a guide for selection of curriculum, speakers, and activities, and it would also become a personal measure for our leaders to evaluate their own growth.

To decide what skills we wanted our leaders to possess, our senior leaders met with the newly established Baptist University board of directors over several months. We began with a lengthy and comprehensive list of qualities, but eventually narrowed the field to ten "leadership core competencies" that we wanted all of our leaders to develop (see Figure 12.2).

Developing these skills has become a major emphasis at our BU sessions and also in the personal evaluation tools that our leaders use. We seek to keep them in front of our leaders in as many ways as possible, and we recognize leaders who are developing and displaying mastery of the core competencies.

FIGURE 12.2 Baptist University Core Competencies

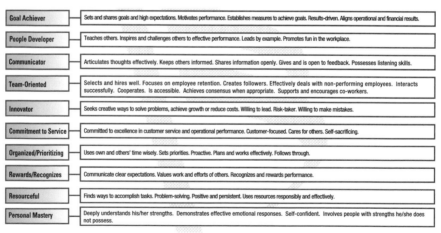

CONTINUED EXPANSION

As we expanded our education programs in an effort to meet the leadership needs of our employees, we began to ask if there were ways to take our leadership training beyond the quarterly Baptist University seminars. The seminars were working wonderfully for our leaders, but the 4,500 employees who were not attending were telling us that they wanted to grow and develop as well. If we were truly going to be a people-developing organization, we needed to equip more than just our 600 leaders; we needed to be teaching and training every employee in our organization.

This conviction led us to develop *Cascade Learning Kits*, a tool that our BU attendees use to train the rest of their staff after each session. At the end of each quarterly meeting, every leader in attendance receives a Cascade Learning Kit covering that day's material. The kits include a script to guide leaders as they talk with their respective staffs, a survey to help evaluate pre- and post-learning needs, and training aids such as handouts and transparencies (see Figure 12.3). Leaders are then held accountable for sharing the information with their staff within the next sixty days, a goal that almost all of our leaders routinely reach. We have been very pleased with the results of this cascade learning technique; our employees appreciate the training they receive, and our leaders enjoy the benefits of a well-trained and educated staff. In addition, because of cascade learning, after a BU session, our 600 leaders leave the session with one consistent message to take back to our entire workforce. I have heard Brian Jones, former Baptist Health Care Director of People Development (now with the Baptist Leadership Institute), say "Cascade learning takes a one-day event and transforms it into teachable moments that move the organization giant leaps all at once."

Another method we have used to expand our educational efforts has been the development of BU core courses, specialty courses and e-learning modules. Core courses and specialty courses are on-campus courses taught periodically throughout the year over a wide range of subjects (see Figure 12.4). E-learning modules, offered through our intranet, also provide opportunities for employees to receive training in numerous areas. We offer courses structured around our ten leadership core competencies in areas such as "Time Management," "Peer Interviewing," and "Reward and Recognition." All of these are simply efforts to make learning and work as intertwined as possible for our employees; we want them to view their training not as a separate activity but as a meaningful vehicle for enhancing job performance.

FIGURE 12.3 Cascade Learning Kits Sample

RESTRUCTURING FOR GROWTH

As our leadership development programs have continued to grow and evolve, several key structural changes have taken place. As I mentioned, we first formed a Baptist University board of directors to oversee our leadership training initiatives. Also, the six subcommittees that had executed the Bridges sessions merged into four new subcommittees: Linkage, Curriculum, Sessions, and Access and Delivery. These subcommittees are responsible for every detail of Baptist University.

The *Curriculum Committee* has the task of developing curriculum not only for each quarterly BU session, but also for our BU core courses, specialty courses, and e-learning modules. Each BU session includes a skill-building work session focusing on the development of a specific competency, and the Curriculum Committee develops these activities. They are also responsible for identifying teachers and facilitators for our sessions. For each quarterly meeting, we bring in a nationally-known expert in some area

FIGURE 12.4 Baptist University Course Catalogue

of management to speak to our leaders, usually concerning one of our five pillars. These speakers have included a service expert from the Ritz Carlton (service), a consultant on employee retention who challenged us all to be Chief Retention Officers in our departments (people), and a business development expert who taught us to think of our department as a growth opportunity (growth). The Curriculum Committee identifies the areas where our people need to grow and finds the best people in the country to help them get there.

The *Sessions Committee* works specifically on our four BU sessions each year, carrying out the curriculum plan provided by the Curriculum Committee, taking care of logistics such as food and parking, and planning celebrations as part of each session. As they did with Bridges, the Sessions

Committee chooses a catchy theme for each quarter and works to create a fun and exciting atmosphere for learning. As a regular part of each BU session, I make a presentation highlighting accomplishments for each of our affiliates, but I don't normally get to do it in a suit and tie. Each quarter, the Sessions Committee dresses me up in a theme-related costume to deliver my presentation. I have taken the stage as an astronaut, a cowboy, and Superman, to name a few (see Figure 12.5). In one recent quarter, I wore a pirate costume with a patch over my eye to go with our Pirates of the Caribbean theme. The employees love it and look forward to seeing what silly costume I will wear the next time. I've been challenged sometimes that this behavior is "not appropriate for a CEO." To which I reply, "You're right. But I'm not trying to be seen as the CEO. I'm trying to be seen as Al."

FIGURE 12.5 Al in Costume at Baptist University

The *Access and Delivery Committee* takes care of logistical issues, including providing for audio/visual needs for BU sessions, tracking employee participation and credit hours accrued, and overseeing the logistics of our intranet and e-learning programs. They have kept all the wheels turning as our programs have grown in size and complexity. The fourth committee, *Linkage*, is responsible for "connecting the dots," establishing links between the information gained at each session and what actually goes on at work each day. They own the cascade accountability process, and live by this motto: "If they don't change, did they really learn?" Their job is to see that the training we do truly makes a difference.

AND THE EVOLUTION CONTINUES . .

The programs and processes I have just described have served us well for the last four years, gaining us national recognition as people developers and, most importantly, equipping our leaders and employees to be the best they can be. However, the same conviction that led us to expand the original Bridges program has now led us to make continuing changes to our Baptist University program. The vision of Baptist University is to be "the best people developer in America." In order to make this vision a reality, and to sustain and grow our success, we must continuously develop *all* of our employees. As effective as our efforts to this point have been, there are still significant portions of our workforce who receive minimal training and development.

We want this to change. We want it so strongly that we have set a corporate goal for all employees to receive at least sixty hours annually of personal growth and development by the year 2008. In order to achieve this goal, in early 2004, Baptist University underwent a major transition, splitting into three colleges: the *College of Leadership Development*, the *College of Performance Excellence*, and the *College of Clinical Excellence*. Each college has its own dean and board of directors, and each targets a different section of our workforce (see Figure 12.6).

While we are still in the beginning stages of this transition, we believe that this is the next stage in our development as a world-class leadership training organization. As Pam Bilbrey has shared, "Whether it is the housekeeper who dreams of becoming an LPN, the nurse who dreams of working in administration, or an entry level staff who dreams of someday becoming a manager, those dreams are out there waiting to be fulfilled.

FIGURE 12.6 Three Colleges within Baptist University

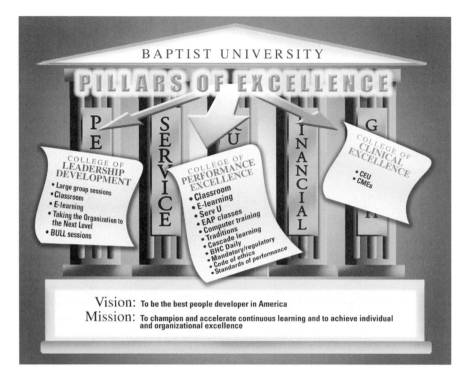

While [the previous Baptist University] structure has been useful in creating a great culture of leadership development, it is time to enhance the dream and help all employees achieve their career goals and be the very best they can be."

The importance of this investment was affirmed to me in August 2003 on the day before one of our BU sessions when I received an e-mail from a leader. Her husband had been a patient at Baptist Hospital. She shared the following

> I am writing as a customer and as a colleague within the Baptist Health Care "family."
>
> I am a nurse; I look hard at healthcare service when I am the customer. I have been skeptical about some things I hear at BU: I found it difficult to relate to the celebration of Baptist excellence. It has been very hard for me to buy into the mantra of "The Best."

Until my husband was your patient!

In the week we were your customers, NOT ONE person missed the mark! Everyone was kind, attentive, competent, genuine. I walked around the facility "feeling" the atmosphere. The bulletin boards shouted out the messages of commitment to excellence, attention to quality care, praise for staff participation in BH initiatives. In the halls and my husband's room on 1 West, I saw numerous examples of staff's comfort in the performance of duties. I gave myself a little tour of some other floors and felt myself noticed, welcomed, offered-help. I asked some nurses on duty if they really liked working here, and they all said, "Yes . . . Well, we have our moments, but I couldn't think of anywhere else I would like to work." I was really amazed!

When I go to BU this week, I will be a better participant! I can relate so much better to the collective enthusiasm demonstrated there! I am glad to be part of this Health Care System!

KEY FIVE

HARDWIRE SUCCESS THROUGH SYSTEMS OF ACCOUNTABILITY

I f you take the tools I've outlined to this point—from critical success factors to service recovery to leadership development- -and put them to work in your organization, I guarantee you will see results. However, without a solid system of accountability in place, you will find those results difficult to sustain. To achieve long-lasting change in your organization, you must help every staff member understand that his or her actions matter—not only for personal achievement but also as a piece of the overall organizational puzzle; you must create owners. Only then are you on your way to "hardwiring" success.

Accountability for *every* employee must be built in to your culture. Far too many employees cringe when they hear the word "accountability" because to them it brings up images of scolding, humiliation, and striving to reach unrealistic goals set by management. That is not the type of accountability you'll find in a WOW! culture. In Chapter 13, Building a Culture that Holds Employees Accountable, I want to share some of the many tools that we use to hold our employees accountable in a way that they desire and appreciate. It has been a critical part of our journey to excellence.

CHAPTER 13

Building a Culture that Holds Employees Accountable

> *The ancient Romans had a tradition: whenever one of their engineers constructed an arch, as the capstone was hoisted into place, the engineer assumed accountability for his work in the most profound way possible: he stood under the arch.*
>
> — -Michael Armstrong

I have shared previously that I am a numbers guy. I love to analyze charts and graphs and to look at our patient satisfaction surveys and budget reports. I care about those numbers because I believe they are important indicators both of our successes and of our opportunities for improvement. Our patient satisfaction surveys tell us not only what we have achieved, but how we can improve for the next time. The same is true for budget and clinical care reports. They are all valuable accountability tools, and they are necessary to establishing a WOW! workplace. However, not all of our employees are "numbers people." Scores and numbers typically do not excite our clinical staff; they get excited about providing great patient care. In order to sell them on the value of accountability, we must demonstrate how using those tools can enhance the quality of their service. When they learn to view accountability as a method for providing excellent service, they will eagerly get on board.

The final key to achieving service and operational excellence is to "Hardwire Success through Systems of Accountability." This includes both formal accountability tools and more informal, day-to-day accountability practices. Employees who know they are responsible for achieving results become owners, and they find the motivation to do what it takes to reach their goals. We have learned a great deal as we have developed our accountability process and have found it extremely effective. While your specific measurement tools may differ from ours, I hope that a description of our accountability process can help you to identify the needs in your organization.

ACHIEVE ALIGNMENT

As you begin to develop systems of accountability, you will have the greatest impact when the results you seek are clearly defined and linked to your critical success factors—in our case, the five pillars of operational excellence. When you have identified your goals, the next step is to seek alignment by clearly communicating them throughout the organization. Goals at every level should reflect the overall goals of the system. There is tremendous power in aligning your workers and leaders in this way.

Setting these systems of accountability in place can be a complex and daunting task. A look at our strategic planning process will provide more insight into the way that we have woven alignment and accountability into the Baptist Health Care culture.

As Figure 13.1 shows, we begin with our mission, vision, and values because we want to keep those ideals at the forefront. As our employees set goals for themselves and their departments, we never want them to forget that we are striving to be "the best health system in America" (our vision) and that integrity, vision, innovation, superior service, stewardship, and teamwork are our core values. Everything that happens in our organization, from senior management meetings to tissue sampling in the lab, should be governed by our mission, vision, and values.

From that foundation, we move directly into our five pillars of operational excellence, or defined critical success factors. All of the goals and targets, short-term and long-term, that we set for our organization are linked to the five pillars. Thus, early in the process, we develop a Core Strategy statement for each pillar. Figure 13.2 lists our core strategies under each pillar for 2003–2004. Each of these core strategies will become the guide for more specific goals to be set under that pillar.

To aid in our goal development process, we bring together leaders from several areas of the organization—including strategic planning, finance,

FIGURE 13.1 Baptist Health Care's Strategic Planning Process

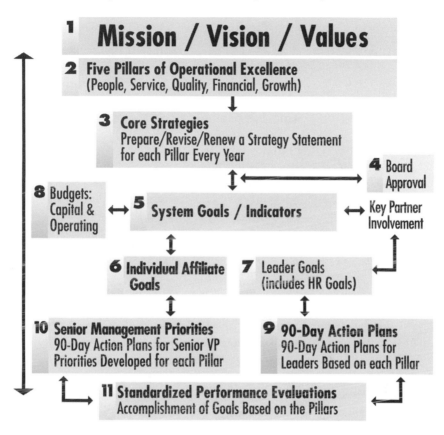

human resources, information services, and patient care—to form a *Strategic Measurement Team*. It's a simple concept, really: We wanted to assemble the people in the organization who have the most responsibility for setting and measuring goals and targets and use their collective talents and insights to develop organizational goals. The Strategic Measurement Team works in coordination with senior officers to develop annual system goals for Baptist Health Care. Although they are updated annually, the system goals include goals and targets not just for the next fiscal year, but typically for a period of three to five years.

The team uses a variety of inputs to establish system goals and presents them annually to the Baptist Health Care Board of Directors for approval *before* each affiliate prepares its annual budget. We want our goals and strategies

FIGURE 13.2 Baptist Health Care Corporation Core Strategies
         2003–2004

People Baptist Health Care should be employer of choice in the market area and a health–care industry leader in values-based recruitment, employee satisfaction, employee retention, and leadership development.

Service Baptist Health Care must provide compassionate care and service to all customers at a level which continues to set the highest standards in the health–care industry.

Quality Baptist Health Care must achieve health–care industry leading results in clinical performance.

Financial Baptist Health Care must optimize financial results while meeting its mission to provide services to all, regardless of ability to pay, and to improve the health status and quality of life for residents of communitites served.

Growth Baptist Health Care must achieve fiscally responsible services for growth in volume and locations while achieving financial targets.

to determine the allocation of our resources, not the other way around. Once they have developed and gained approval for Baptist Health Care system goals, the Strategic Measurement Team works with administrators and leaders responsible for operations at each entity to prepare affiliate-specific goals and strategies. These goals both come out of and roll up to our Baptist Health Care system-wide goals, and they are set to foster continuous improvement in each of the pillar categories.

For example, under the Quality pillar, the 2005 system goal for "medication event rates" (measuring the incidence of medication errors) is 2.7 per 10,000 doses. Each hospital and nursing home has its own goal for "medication event rates" that will enable us to reach our system goal. In order for Baptist Health Care to reach its overall goal, each affiliate must meet or exceed its related goal. Under the Financial pillar, each Baptist Health Care affiliate has targets for operating margin that must be met in order for Baptist Health Care to reach its corporate goal. For the Service pillar, the system goal is to achieve the ninety-ninth percentile in customer satisfaction for all areas measured; therefore, each facility now sets a goal to reach the ninety-ninth percentile. In this way, each affiliate organization is working to accomplish its own unique goals while also effectively working to accomplish the overall goals of Baptist Health Care. This alignment is invaluable.

When each Baptist Health Care affiliate has finalized their linked but unique set of system goals for the upcoming year, each individual leader throughout the organization then develops a set of annual goals for his or her department, again by pillar category, that are connected to the goals for Baptist Health Care and for their own entity. With these goals, the leader identifies actions that he or she and the department can take during the course of the year to help accomplish the overall goals of the organization. Achieving the ninety-ninth percentile in patient satisfaction is no longer just Baptist Health Care's goal, or even Baptist Hospital's—now the Nursing Leader for Obstetrics is personally responsible for reaching the ninety-ninth percentile, and she can clearly see how her department's achievement ties in and contributes to hospital- and system-wide goals (see Figure 13.3).

Leaders develop these goals in collaboration with their direct supervisor and are held accountable for results through the use of ninety-day action plans discussed in this chapter. Using these plans, leaders and their reporting seniors assess their progress toward goal achievement on a real-time basis. Finally, leader annual performance evaluations are also structured by pillar and linked directly to the accomplishment of individual leader goals. This process assures that all leaders are contributing to the accomplishment of common goals in the manner most appropriate for them and also ties their short-term performance to the achievement of longer-term goals for the organization.

Nurse leader Lynn Pierce appreciates the perspective that this strategic planning process provides. "With accountability, you have to create an environment so that leaders can see the big picture. Early on, the dots were never connected for us. It just felt like people throwing ideas out there. We

FIGURE 13.3 How Annual Goals Cascade Throughout the Organization

Service Pillar: Baptist Health Care must provide compassionate care and service to all customers at a level which continues to set the highest standards in the healthcare industry			
Yearly Goals:	2004	2006	2008
Baptist Health Care: Achieve the following results in patient satisfaction across all areas measured (aggregate percentile rankings)	99th	99th	99th
Baptist Hospital, Inc: Achieve the following results in patient satisfaction tools utilized: Inpatient	99th	99th	99th
Baptist Hospital Department: Achieve the following results in patient satisfaction: Nursing Category for Obstetrics / 3E	99th	99th	99th

rebelled as leaders until we could see the big picture." Our strategic planning process creates alignment throughout every level of the organization and helps all of our employees to see how their actions make a difference.

EMPOWER EMPLOYEES

We like to refer to our management style at Baptist Health Care as "tight, loose, tight." First, we are "tight" in establishing and clearly communicating goals and targets; we make our expectations clear up front. But we are "loose" in terms of controlling the methods leaders use to accomplish those goals. As long as leaders comply with our standards of performance, they have great freedom in the approach they use to address problems and achieve results. While there are some methods and tools that are non-negotiable because we know they work (e.g., ninety-day action plans, communication boards, reward and recognition, nurse leader rounding), many problem-solving and service-enhancing decisions are left up to our leaders. Finally, we are "tight" in our expectations. We expect our leaders and departments to accomplish the goals that they have set. Tight, loose, tight.

At Baptist Health Care, our ninety-day action plans—which serve as the basic building block of our accountability process—reflect this "tight, loose, tight" style of management. They take alignment one step further, requiring leaders to now set individual goals that reflect entity and system goals, but they also provide employees the freedom and support to achieve the goals they set.

Once a leader's individual annual goals have been approved, the next step is to prepare a shorter term action plan. We have found that a ninety-day time frame is long enough to get things done, but still short enough to foster real-time accountability. Therefore, we ask all of our leaders to prepare action plans every ninety days at the beginning of each quarter.

Typically no more than two-pages long, the plan spells out what that leader can accomplish in the next ninety days to assure that he or she is on track to accomplish overall goals for the year. While the ninety-day action plan holds our staff accountable for achieving results, it is also flexible enough to allow them to make changes when the need arises. Leaders meet with their supervisors at least once a quarter to track progress and make adjustments as necessary.

Not surprisingly, our ninety-day action plans are divided into five sections, one for each pillar category. Under each pillar, the plan lists established goals and the action steps necessary to accomplish those goals. Finally, the action plan includes a column for a ninety-day result report, where leaders note their progress toward achieving each goal (see Figure 13.4).

We have found that ninety-day action plans work very effectively to encourage communication between a leader and his or her direct supervisor. By working together to determine feasible goals and action steps, they establish a relationship built on clear expectations. Many business books refer to this process of leader communication and negotiation regarding goals and results as "managing up." This practice empowers our leaders and strengthens morale by establishing healthy, working relationships between leaders and supervisors across our organization.

At the end of each year, on a form that mirrors their ninety-day action plans, leaders receive a leader performance evaluation, which basically measures the degree to which they have accomplished their individual set of goals for the year. Using action plans as a basis for annual evaluations has advantages for both leaders and supervisors. First, since goals on the action plan are set by leaders themselves, they can never say that they were unaware of expectations. Second, since goals on ninety-day action plans must be measurable, supervisors have clear, objective data with which to complete their evaluations; they can never be accused of subjectivity.

FIGURE 13.4 Ninety-Day Action Plan

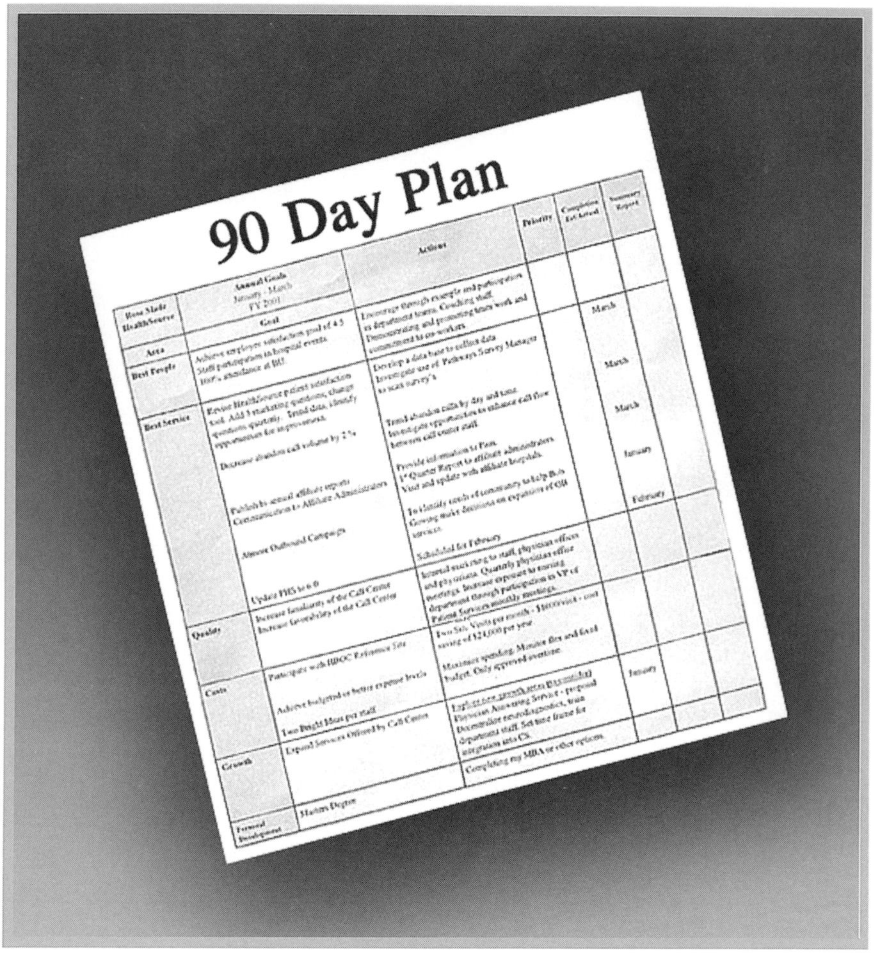

Two other accountability tools that appear regularly on ninety-day action plans are the *Budget Accountability Report* (BAR) and the *Clinical Accountability Report of Excellence* (CARE). As we began to get serious about holding departments and individuals accountable, we discovered a problem: The tools that we were using to measure financial performance and clinical quality were far too complex and time-consuming to do our department leaders much good. Our clinical quality reports measured over 400 indicators, and the budget report was just as complicated. While the information was all there, our leaders did not have the time to study the details of those reports to find the problem issues related to their departments. They had departments to run!

Our department leaders needed a brief, concise report that could quickly tell them how they were doing related to the budget and to clinical quality. We became even more aware of this need for a quality indicator when a Baldrige examiner asked us, "What is your single measure of quality?" At the time, we didn't have one, but we knew that we needed it if we were going to hold our leaders accountable for quality.

The beauty of the BAR and CARE, which were created at Baptist Health Care, is that they can very quickly tell a leader or supervisor how a department is doing in key budget and quality areas. Both use the same 100-point scale to evaluate performance, and they measure the most important indicators in each area. The BAR calculates how well a department is doing based on its budget for three areas—revenue dollars, major expense categories (which will differ by department), and full-time employees (or equivalents)—and creates a one-number score to show their performance. A score of 80 means the department is exactly on budget; a 100 means they are doing ten percent better than budget, and a 60 means they're ten percent under. Almost all of our department leaders have a target BAR score under the financial section of their ninety-day action plans, and their supervisors can look at the report and tell immediately whether they are making budget or not. Leaders feel a great sense of accountability for their department's BAR score; if they turn in a score of less than 80, they must also turn in a ninety-day action plan showing how they plan to raise the score (see Figure 13.5).

The Clinical Accountability Report of Excellence works very similarly, measuring clinical quality instead of financial performance. To determine a department's CARE score, we take that department's most important measures of quality and roll them into one number. We use the same 100-point scale, but in order to earn an 80, the department must be doing ten percent better than they did the previous year. To earn a 100, the clinical result has to be world class. For example, in a world class hospital, how many patients will get a bed sore? Zero. How many patients will fall out of bed? Zero. How many times will the surgical staff check the correct limb before operating? Every time. So in order to earn a 100 score for any indicator, the result has to be perfect all of the time. That makes our departments' average CARE scores of 92 to 95 even more impressive. Again, target CARE scores appear regularly on ninety-day action plans, under the quality pillar.

FIGURE 13.5 Budget Accountability Report

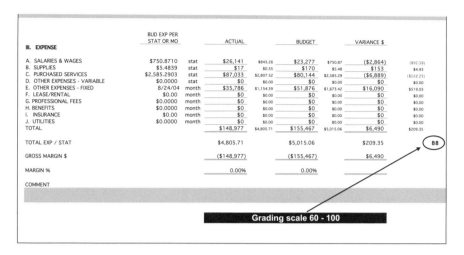

III. EXPENSE	BUD EXP PER STAT OR MO		ACTUAL		BUDGET		VARIANCE $	
A. SALARIES & WAGES	$750.8710	stat	$26,141	$843.26	$23,277	$750.87	($2,864)	($92.39)
B. SUPPLIES	$5.4839	stat	$17	$0.55	$170	$5.48	$153	$4.93
C. PURCHASED SERVICES	$2,585.2903	stat	$87,033	$2,807.52	$80,144	$2,585.29	($6,889)	($222.23)
D. OTHER EXPENSES - VARIABLE	$0.0000	stat	$0	$0.00	$0	$0.00	$0	$0.00
E. OTHER EXPENSES - FIXED	8/24/04	month	$35,786	$1,154.39	$51,876	$1,673.42	$16,090	$519.03
F. LEASE/RENTAL	$0.00	month	$0	$0.00	$0	$0.00	$0	$0.00
G. PROFESSIONAL FEES	$0.0000	month	$0	$0.00	$0	$0.00	$0	$0.00
H. BENEFITS	$0.0000	month	$0	$0.00	$0	$0.00	$0	$0.00
I. INSURANCE	$0.00	month	$0	$0.00	$0	$0.00	$0	$0.00
J. UTILITIES	$0.0000	month	$0	$0.00	$0	$0.00	$0	$0.00
TOTAL			$148,977	$4,805.71	$155,467	$5,015.06	$6,490	$209.35
TOTAL EXP / STAT			$4,805.71		$5,015.06		$209.35	88
GROSS MARGIN $			($148,977)		($155,467)		$6,490	
MARGIN %			0.00%		0.00%			
COMMENT								

Grading scale 60 - 100

I have described these two tools to illustrate this principle: When you decide to hold your staff accountable for performance, you must provide accountability tools that they can understand and use. Telling our employees to stick to budget was one thing, but showing them exactly where they were overspending was quite another. Nurse Leader Kelly Rozier shared, "On our nursing unit, we just did not have a clue about spending money. I said, 'There's no way I'm spending this much,' but when we started using the BAR, I could see exactly where the money was going, and I learned so much in the process." Providing tools that show employees exactly where they stand empowers them to improve their own performance and hold themselves and their coworkers accountable for being the best.

MEASURE IN REAL TIME

As we journeyed through the process of cultural transformation, we began to enjoy the fruits of aligned goals, established systems of accountability, and empowered leaders. We also quickly realized that the sooner that information and data reports were received, the more effective leaders became in making needed adjustments.

Our patient satisfaction results are an excellent example. Before 1995, we received quarterly reports from Press, Ganey and Associates. These reports came in about forty-five days after the quarter had ended, meaning that some of the information in the report was over four months old! We often couldn't even remember what had been going on during the last quarter that would have affected our patient satisfaction scores, and there was very little we could do to improve anything that far after the fact.

We had asked our leaders to commit to providing world-class service to our customers, and they communicated that quarterly reports did not permit them to do this. They simply could not make the needed changes in time to achieve high-level results with four-month-old patient satisfaction reports.

Eventually, we developed the system that is still in place today. Every Thursday at 3 P.M. in the afternoon, we receive an e-mail tabulation of our patient satisfaction survey results for the week, and those results are quickly circulated to every part of the organization. The report shows two things: (1) weekly patient satisfaction results by unit and by survey question, and (2) results needed (also by unit and survey question) to achieve the ninety-ninth percentile, and thus meet our overall goal. When there is a problem, we can address it immediately, and we can tell within a week if we have made progress.

If the weekly report, such as the one in Figure 13.6, shows that results for a question about "room cleanliness" have fallen below target, leaders who are accountable for room cleanliness immediately begin to identify possible causes and make changes to improve scores. If the lower scores persist, those leaders will be asked to develop a ninety-day plan for more specific corrective action. We also recognize the department with the most favorable results. That department gains possession for the week of our roving patient satisfaction trophy. We have found that the closer to real-time our results are communicated, the more our performance improves. Real-time measurement eliminates many excuses and makes true accountability possible.

In addition to this weekly report, we also review patient satisfaction surveys daily, as soon as they come in. Results from each day's surveys are e-mailed to appropriate department leaders so that they can immediately address a problem. If a patient gives us a score of three or lower (out of a five-point scale), we make a personal phone call to that patient to find out what we could have done to provide very good care. Baptist Hospital Administrator Bob Murphy appreciates the immediate accountability that this brings: "Daily review of patient satisfaction surveys allows us to do a 'temperature check' every day to make sure we're on target."

FIGURE 13.6 Excerpt from the Weekly Patient Satisfaction Report

May 14 - 20, 2004

		Scores Week Ending May 14 - May 20 n = 40	Scores Week Ending May 7 - May 13 n = 50	Scores this Month Mar 31 - Apr 29 n = 133
	BAPTIST HOSPITAL INPATIENT WEEKLY SURVEY ALL ITEMS			
A	Admission	93.4	91.3	92.6
	Percentile	99%	99%	99%
B	Room	88.6	87.2	88.3
	Percentile	99%	99%	99%
C	Meals	89.6	86.1	88.0
	Percentile	99%	99%	99%
D	Nurses	94.4	90.7	93.7
	Percentile	99%	96%	99%
E	Tests & Treatments	93.0	92.0	91.9
	Percentile	99%	99%	99%
F	Visitors & Family	93.1	92.6	92.5
	Percentile	99%	99%	99%
G	Physician	94.4	93.2	93.0
	Percentile	99%	99%	99%
H	Discharge	92.1	89.9	90.4
	Percentile	99%	99%	99%
I	Personal Issues	95.1	90.4	92.7
	Percentile	99%	99%	99%
J	Overall Assessment	94.7	91.3	93.1
	Percentile	99%	96%	99%
	Overall Hospital Rating	92.6	90.4	91.5
	Percentile	99%	99%	99%
	QTR to Date - Overall Hospital Rating			**90.2**
	Percentile			**99%**
	Month-to-Date Return Rate			**29%**

Distribution of Responses for the week:

Very Poor	Poor	Fair	Good	Very Good
1.4%	0.8%	2.7%	14.3%	81.1%

Distribution Goal:

1%	<2%	<5%	<20%	>70%

Real-time measurement also raises the level of intensity. For example, after five years of consistently ranking in the ninety-ninth percentile in patient satisfaction, for one quarter in 2003 Baptist Hospital dropped to the ninety-seventh percentile. As soon as those results came in, our whole workforce responded. Everyone, from volunteers to employees to management, turned things up a notch. We organized "back-to-basics" classes and did everything we could think of to get back into the ninety-ninth percentile, which we achieved by the next quarter. Our employees have established incredibly high expectations for themselves, and giving them immediate feedback enables them to consistently maintain those world-class standards.

While it isn't possible to measure and report on all key measures on a daily or weekly basis, we have established a policy of trying to report key data as close to real-time as possible. I encourage you to do the same. It helps motivate leaders, cuts down on excuses, and improves overall performance. Real-time measurement also enables you to give timely rewards to recognize exemplary performance—another key reason to hardwire accountability into your culture.

REWARD AND RECOGNIZE

One of our most effective—and fun—accountability practices is reward and recognition. I believe that our emphasis on celebration has been as effective as any specific measurement tool in establishing a culture that supports and embraces accountability. By recognizing and rewarding outstanding performance, we make accountability a positive concept for our employees rather than a negative, punitive idea. I outlined our reward and recognition methods in Chapter 8, Celebrating Successes through Reward and Recognition, emphasizing the importance of celebration in employee retention. Here I want to share how it can also play a vital role in accountability.

The power of positive reinforcement is an often underestimated force. Small perks, such as an "employee of the month" parking spot, have motivated many workers to exceed the regular demands of their jobs in hope of gaining recognition. We have found that by encouraging our leaders to spend more time "catching" their staff doing things right than correcting them for doing things wrong, we enhance accountability at every level.

At Baptist Health Care, we want to provide so much motivation to do the right things that our employees will modify their own behaviors when necessary. One way that we can do that is by reinforcing every good behavior that we see. When a food service employee receives a handwritten note from her hospital administrator thanking her for outstanding service, she is very likely to maintain or even improve her level of service. When nurses know that their supervisors will be notified when they are mentioned for exceeding expectations on a patient satisfaction survey, they will work a little harder to provide excellent care. When coworkers have the authority to give WOW! awards to each other, they will look for actions and behaviors to reward.

In a WOW! culture, employees are held accountable for the good and the bad. We want to celebrate every individual, departmental, and organizational achievement to let our staff know that we appreciate their efforts. And when results fall below expectations, we want to partner with employees to find the quickest and most effective way to bring that performance back to an acceptable level.

Aligned systems of accountability, empowered employees, real-time measurement, and reward and recognition are all drivers of performance improvement. Leaders will respond positively to an accountability process that clearly makes known what is expected of them and helps them to see how meeting those expectations contributes to their success, and that of their coworkers and the organization as a whole. Those employees know how to win, and why they want to. That provides incentive to do the right things, at the right time, for the right reasons. They also understand that they will receive the resources and support needed to succeed because achieving their targeted results will help the organization accomplish its goals. Doing these things will create a positive accountability system in your organization that facilitates continuous improvement and gets a WOW! response from your customers and employees.

CHAPTER 14

Beyond Baptist Health Care: Other Systems on the Journey to WOW!

We must get beyond textbooks, go out into the bypaths... and tell the world the glories of our journey.
—John Hope Franklin

As I said at the beginning of this book, I am indeed a most fortunate man. The privilege I have had to be surrounded by the dedicated, committed, creative, talented team of employees that make up Baptist Health Care is a gift that I do not take for granted. In fact, our entire team feels a great sense of responsibility to take the remarkable results that we have achieved and "share the gospel" with an industry desperately looking for some good news. These are challenging times for the healthcare industry. Leaders face reimbursement difficulties, aging workforce, aging physical plants, and a baby boomer generation that is fast approaching a time when they will become heavy utilizers of healthcare services. The industry is looking for something to engage and energize its workforce and to attract and bring in new young talent. We believe creating a WOW! culture can be a significant piece to solving that puzzle.

To that end, for the last seven years, we have been actively sharing our results and methodologies with other organizations. As more and more of our colleagues from around the country contacted us and said, "We want to try to duplicate the results you are achieving at Baptist Health Care," we became eager to find a way to help. So we began to put together a structure to help organizations learn from us. We have now had over 6,000 health-care workers, representing approximately one-third of the hospitals and health systems in the country, come to Pensacola for that purpose. As we work to equip these organizations, they return the favor by motivating and inspiring our workforce. The bulletin board pictured in Figure 14.1 reminds our employees that they are making a difference for healthcare systems everywhere. We are able to tell our employees, "Not only are you making a difference right here in Pensacola, but you are literally changing the way health care is practiced all over this country."

Through our Baptist Leadership Institute (BLI), we provide a broad array of services to health systems and other organizations that are at various stages on the journey to WOW! Those services include hosting onsite benchmarking visits to our hospital campuses, providing speakers for board retreats and leadership training sessions, making materials such as our Best Practices Series (www.BaptistLeadershipInstitute.com), and providing multiyear consulting engagements to help organizations that really want to fast-track the process. Ten times a year, we also offer a two-day seminar—structured around the same five keys I have presented in this book—titled "Creating a Culture that Inspires the Workforce" (see Figure 14.2). I cannot tell you how many times people have told me, "Well, that works for you at Baptist, but we are different because _____." I'm amazed by the justifications we can find to explain away poor results. We did it before our transformation, and I hear it from others today. What BLI has to offer is not a silver bullet. In fact, as anyone who has read this far can see, creating a healthy culture takes a lot of hard work, but the biggest step is the first

FIGURE 14.1 Benchmark Groups

FIGURE 14.2 Seminar Provided by Baptist Leadership Institute

one—acknowledging that the culture can be healthier and that our organization will only be as great as we decide to make it.

To help drive home the fact that WOW! results can be achieved at any organization whose leadership commits to making it happen, I would like to share the stories of three organizations that we have consulted over the last two years as they have begun their journey. I hope you will see from these examples that neither location, size, nor organizational complexity are legitimate excuses for delaying the start of your cultural transformation. I have chosen three organizations that are quite distinct from one another. One is a single hospital in Florence, South Carolina. The second is large, multihospital system with over 10,000 employees serving a five-county area in northern Atlanta. The third is a three-hospital system with approximately 1,800 employees in Sarnia, Canada.

CAROLINAS HEALTH SYSTEM, FLORENCE, SOUTH CAROLINA

The Carolinas Health System was formed as the result of a merger of two hospitals in Florence that were later merged into one community-based hospital. That hospital is now owned by Triad Hospitals, Inc., based in Dallas, Texas. Jim O'Loughlin, the CEO of Carolinas, describes the factors that led him to believe that they needed to make some changes:

> The first was we were still struggling to combine the cultures from the two original hospitals. As we assessed our market, we recognized that we were in a very competitive market and struggling to find a way to distinguish ourselves from our competitors. Our hospital was only six years old and, despite that, did not have a good reputation in the community. There was a period of time when we were trying to cut costs, staffing was short, and the overall reputation, even among the employees, was that this was not the place to come if you were sick. We shared with our workforce that you can have the nicest facilities and the most advanced equipment, but if your employees do not feel good about working in the hospital, it does not matter how nice a facility is.

Their competitor is a strong, well-financed facility, and Jim and his team felt the need for some way to distinguish themselves. Just as we decided in 1995 to make service excellence our competitive battleground, so did Carolinas in 2003.

Jim and his team reached the conclusion that customer service as a business practice is falling by the wayside. Consequently, those companies that are willing to provide exemplary service will have a significant competitive advantage. They assessed the status of their organization and decided that they were in a position to give this effort the management focus that it would need to be successful. His first and biggest surprise as they began their journey was how readily the Carolinas employees embraced the change. (I remember experiencing the same degree of surprise when we received our employee satisfaction survey results eighteen months into our transformation.) Jim had anticipated having to fight the attitude that said, "Well, this is just another program of the month, and administration will soon move on to something else, so we'll just bide our time and get through it." That never occurred at Carolinas. For the most part, and to the great pleasure of the management team, employees eagerly embraced this new service excellence culture. As a result, the workforce actually helped drive the change.

A real delight at Carolinas has been to see employees in the hospital that had not previously served in formal leadership roles becoming engaged and serving on various committees. It has provided an opportunity for competent people to step into leadership roles and actively create positive change. Jim believes they were able to tap into many employees' hidden strengths when they began engaging them on committees and service teams. He says, "Seeing somebody who is a nondegreed person that is typically in more of a support function taking a leadership role has been a pleasant surprise." Employees from their housekeeping staff, for example, serving on committees, talking about customer service, and leading other professionals is an extremely effective and unusual role reversal.

In the relatively short time that Carolinas has been on this journey, they have produced documented results. They were extremely pleased at the recent annual Triad meeting to be recognized as one of the top hospitals in the Triad system based on five criteria: (1) patient satisfaction, (2) employee satisfaction, (3) physician satisfaction, (4) community involvement, and (5) financial performance. To be identified as a top hospital, they had to rank in the top ten percent in all three satisfaction results. They have made great strides toward reaching their vision—to be the best hospital in South Carolina—already rising from the fiftieth to the ninety-fifth percentile. However, Jim says they will not be satisfied until they reach the ninety-ninth.

He and his staff have clearly seen the needle move as the culture has changed at Carolinas. Employees now understand the tremendous role that attitude plays in service excellence. In fact, he says the word is getting out that a certain type of attitude is required in order to work at Carolinas. They lost some skilled clinical people as they began this journey, just as we did at Baptist, because management became convinced that employee attitudes had to be consistent if results were going to be consistent. They have put together a video that they use to clearly communicate expectations early in the hiring process. In the early stages of the application process, candidates are discouraged from following through if they are not willing to commit to the "Carolinas Difference" of interacting with their patients and coworkers.

One of the ways they have tried to establish sustainability in the program is by creating an accountability tool called the directors' dashboard. The dashboard enables them to hold directors accountable for their performance each quarter. For instance, directors are required to provide top management with the names of at least five percent of the people of their department so that thank-you notes can be written. They are also required to attend at least seventy-five percent of all the "town hall meetings." The dashboard keeps track of directors' progress toward these goals. They have created a dashboard for all of the different initiatives that they learned through the Baptist Leadership Institute and they examine it each quarter. They have even created a point system for the dashboard that is directly linked to the organization's incentive compensation plan. This did not happen without some resistance. He notes that the term "micromanagement" has been thrown back at management because most managers are not used to this degree of accountability. His response has been, "If you don't measure it, you don't pay attention to it, and if it is important to us, then we are spending our time on it and you are going to be held accountable for it."

The biggest question Jim had as they embarked was, "Will this be a sustainable end product?" He notes that one of the reasons they decided to engage the Baptist Leadership Institute was because of the long-term sustainable results that they had seen Baptist achieve. That is what they wanted—not just a flash in the pan. He believes that the "Carolinas Difference" has become so embedded into their culture that it supersedes him or any other leader. They are committed to sticking to this journey, even if financial struggles or other challenges may tempt them to give up, because they believe they will continue to see the WOW! results that they have already begun to achieve.

WELLSTAR HEALTH SYSTEM, MARIETTA, GEORGIA

Shifting to the south a bit, I'd like to describe another organization's attempt to transform their culture. Kim Menefee serves as Vice President of Organizational Development and Public Affairs for WellStar Health System in Marietta, Georgia, and she shared with me some of the experiences they have had. The WellStar system consists of five community-owned hospitals and offers numerous other services including hospice, home care, senior facilities, and a fitness center. They have approximately 10,000 employees, plus over 350 physicians and advanced practitioners, and serve a five-county area around northwest Atlanta.

In February 2002, when Dr. Robert Lipson assumed the role of President and CEO of the WellStar system, he led the organization to look at a ten-year horizon and establish strategic imperatives to ensure their ability to meet their mission. Their team established a vision to deliver world-class health care and determined that if they were going to achieve that vision they needed to deliver an "optimal patient experience." Thus, they elected to make customer service one of the defining factors of their success. Kim shared that they were operating from a position of strength in that they were in a growth-oriented area and were already the busiest and largest healthcare system in the greater Atlanta area. Not wanting to waste their prominent market position, they set out to establish a culture that would deliver a service experience so spectacular that WellStar would be the obvious choice for healthcare in their area. With this new direction—and lofty set of goals—came the realization that the culture was going to have to change.

They got started much the same way we did in 1995, by looking for someone to benchmark. They brought a team down to Pensacola in early summer of 2002 and recognized that although our systems were not necessarily alike, we had faced similar challenges. We both had older community hospitals, definitely not the newest, latest, and greatest in relation to our facilities; we both had longevity in our communities but were facing strong, competitive forces. When they observed firsthand the transformation Baptist had gone through, they said, "Your challenges don't seem any different from ours, so if you can transform your culture, then with your help, even though we are larger in size, we can certainly take hold and move our organization forward successfully."

A major factor in their early success was bringing board members and senior leadership together from the beginning. Shortly after our Baptist Learning Institute consultants began working with them, they brought all of the leaders under the WellStar umbrella—about 400 directors, managers, and leaders—together to lay out the strategic plan and vision of the organization. Kim expressed that she was extremely nervous about having to justify the financial impact of taking all those people offline for a day. Wow! Were they blown away with the impact of bringing those leaders together. Kim said that there were people who may have talked on the phone but had never been face-to-face who were able to connect for the first time. This initial gathering drove home the value of effective communication vehicles at WellStar, and they have continued to emphasize communication as they have grown and developed.

They began embedding these new expectations into their system by taking the tools that BLI made available and customizing them for their own organization. Kim says these steps began to create a sense of "systemness" that never existed before. It has added an element of enhanced communication, and enhanced relationships, where people feel more fulfilled with one another coming to work every day. Kim has observed a greater sense of loyalty within the organization as employees see the value in working for WellStar versus one of their competitors in the Atlanta market. "Implementing the things we have learned through our engagement with BLI has energized our organization. WellStar is alive and I don't know if I would have said that even two years ago. By that I mean that every strategic initiative we have is creating excitement within the organization. The enhanced level of communication is bringing our workforce into the process and has made them feel more a part of it. They are excited to work for our organization. I think one of the key points that BLI taught us," Kim said, "is that it's not always about patient satisfaction. You have to engage the hearts of your employees, and I think making that prevalent and communicating it in our organization has been meaningful."

In the one year that WellStar has been engaged with BLI and focused on this cultural revolution, they have already seen patient satisfaction scores trending upward. They have not met their goal, but they are moving in the right direction. They are at the critical accountability stage, putting ninety-day action plans in place, holding people accountable for their scores, and creating actionable implementation plans that will improve their scores. There is also a very strong realization that this cultural emphasis is not going to go away. One of the things they are working on is a tool to make rounding and scripting and all the prescriptive strategies that this book talked about roll up into an accountability report card. They believe that using these best practices will contribute to their success.

One final point that Kim made was the necessity of having a CEO who "walks the talk." Employees respond when they know that the CEO is there supporting the culture change, not just passively, but in an engaged, invigorated manner. Even though WellStar is just at the nine-month mark of this journey, their experience so far leads them to believe that this is a sustainable new way of doing business.

BLUEWATER HEALTH SYSTEM, SARNIA, CANADA

I include the story of Bluewater Health for two reasons. First, they are a heavily unionized organization, but they have refused to use that as an excuse for not attempting to create the kind of environment it takes to deliver great service. Second, they are in Canada and I find it interesting that they face the same kinds of cultural issues and have the same opportunities for improvement as their counterparts in the United States.

The Bluewater Health System was formed in 1996 by a government edict combining a Catholic hospital, a public hospital in Sarnia, and a nearby rural hospital into one system. The government arbitrarily named one CEO for the three hospitals, but left three separate boards in place. Seven years later, in April 2003, after successfully merging the three boards and creating one true system with approximately 1,800 employees, the organization was still floundering with the remnants of the three original cultures.

As their leadership team considered their needs, two common goals formed the impetus to cultural change. The first was a commitment to doing whatever it took to improve their patient satisfaction scores. The second was a desire to become an employer of choice.

Dave Vigar, CEO of Bluewater Health, shared that, "We are right on the border of Michigan, so there are multiple opportunities for people to continue to actually live in Canada and go to the States, where the dollar difference is significant, and use their professions there. So, obviously, we wanted to try to reverse that trend. We looked across our own country and found some organizations doing well on one of those elements. They may do well on patient satisfaction but they have morale issues, or they did really well on morale issues but the patient satisfaction scores had not moved as dramatically as we wanted to see. Some of our folks heard about Baptist Health Care at the Catholic Hospital Association of Canada and we sent people down to see what it was about. Over time, we sent a lot of people down, board members and union members and staff leaders and you seemed to have the right combination. You had been able to accomplish both of those goals, which were what we wanted to do. So we elected to work with the Baptist Leadership Institute."

Dave shared that they clearly recognized on their visits to Pensacola that we had not dealt with a unionized environment in our own transformation, while Bluewater is ninety-five percent unionized. He also refused to let his organization use that as an excuse. He decided to roll the dice and take all of his union leaders down to Pensacola. He brought those nine leaders to our two-day seminar "Creating a Culture that Inspires the Workforce" so that they could see clearly what they sought to accomplish. At the end of the two days, those leaders left Pensacola completely supportive of the new initiative and direction for Bluewater, saying, "This is what we want to see out of our leaders. This is the kind of change our leaders need to make to improve our workplace." According to Dave, that investment was one of the most important ones that he made. He also brought board members to Pensacola so that they could catch the vision for transformation and found it very helpful to have them fully on board when they began to make changes.

Even before coming to Pensacola, Bluewater began engaging their frontline staff in developing "quality of work life initiatives," which created an openness to the idea of cultural revolution. When they presented the idea, the staff immediately got behind it. There was a ground swell of support from both frontline staff and from the board. Upon reflection, Dave admits that they could have included the middle leadership group more effectively early on. "They bought into it fairly quickly, but we had done more work with the grass roots level and at the top with the board. We should have focused more on the middle managers because they are the leaders of this change process."

Dave's role evolved from initiator to brakeman as his staff became energized and engaged to the point where he was having to say, "Slow down." There was so much initial enthusiasm for the change that senior leadership was unprepared to oversee the new initiatives and still deal with their regular, day-to-day issues. He was amazed at how quickly staff responded to the opportunity to get engaged in a positive work environment. Educating their union leaders and having them come back and tell the workforce, "This is a good thing. We need to hold senior management accountable to make this happen" was a powerful driver of their transformation. Interestingly, just a few months into this new focus, senior managers found that frontline staff were holding them accountable for making the kinds of changes they had promised. In other words, employees wanted to know if their leadership team was going to walk the talk. The change in the attitude and atmosphere of the organization was palpable.

As they began to implement some of our best practices, they quickly saw results. Dave shared a personal testimony of both the effectiveness and the enjoyment of rounding. "It is not a hard thing to do once you get into it, and it is very rewarding for me. I find when I am having a bad day, if I'll just get out and visit with my staff, it makes me feel good." He also voiced many of the same feelings I have had regarding the incredible creativity that flows from an engaged workforce. He said he has marveled at the level of energy that employees will give to a cause they believe in. "These are adults that are engaged in your community, they run your service clubs, they have mortgages, they do all these things. They are very creative, but we sometimes have a tendency to label them just as a nurse or a technician or whatever. We forget that they have so much talent and are very well-educated people. We sometimes do not utilize them in the best way we can. It actually was a reward for them to get engaged in something that they don't do as a regular course of their duties."

Bluewater is beginning to see improvement in their patient satisfaction scores, and Dave is confident that with the support of BLI the cultural structure they are striving for is both attainable and sustainable. "The ability to pick up the phone and call someone at Baptist and say, 'Hey, there is something wrong here, can you help us fine tune this?' is a wonderful asset."

Three different stories, three different starting points, one central focus and commitment. A senior management team that made the commitment, engaged their workforce, quit making excuses, and said, "Let's get started. We can—and must—change for the better the environment that our employees come to work in every day. We must do that so that our workforce can unite with us to create a culture that WOWs."

We are encouraged to see the number of senior managers across all industries who are beginning to grasp the power of the principles that have brought us success and apply them in their workplace. It is our deepest desire that you will take away something from this book that will improve the lives of the workers in your business and the customers whom you serve. Together we can build a level of service that is unequaled in the world. Let's do it.

APPENDIX

What about the Physicians?

As I have presented the story of our success in creating this WOW! culture to healthcare leaders around the country, one question that inevitably comes from the audience is, "What about the physicians?" People are eager to know how we have engaged our medical staff—who are not technically our employees, but still have powerful influence over our patients' satisfaction—in our cultural makeover. We have found that a requirement to fulfilling the third key, "Commit to Service Excellence," is to convince the physicians associated with our organization to join us in our quest to be number one.

From the description I gave of our service teams in Chapter 9, Maintaining Quality through Service Teams, you will recall that we have had a team dedicated to our physicians since day one. What was originally the Physician Satisfaction team has now become the *Physician Loyalty* team, but their job has remained basically the same: Do whatever it takes to engage physicians in our cultural transformation.

We are in a nonacademic medical setting, which means that our physician relationships are between independent small business men and women and the hospital. Baptist Health Care, like many health systems in the 1990s, went through a period of acquiring physician practices, primarily in order to prepare for the managed care challenges that were predicted to change the way healthcare was practiced in the United States. As we are all aware, this prediction did not come to pass and many organizations across the country, Baptist Health Care included, decided to abandon this failed strategy. This change of strategic direction made it even more critical that we find a way to positively engage our physicians in the new winning culture that we had created for our workforce and patients.

The hospital–physician relationship has changed tremendously over the last decade. Physicians are finding themselves working harder, and increasingly more isolated from each other and from the healthcare organization at which they practice. A recent study showed that eight-seven percent of physicians say that their overall morale is lower today than it was five years ago. The spirit of volunteerism that used to prevail among physicians has disappeared. They now fully expect to be paid to perform medical staff functions that ten years ago they would gladly have performed at no charge. In order to maintain their income levels, they find themselves more and more drawn into direct competition with the healthcare organization at which they practice. My best friend in college used to say that "Chivalry is not dead, just those that practice it." If we substitute "physician loyalty" for "chivalry" in that assessment, I'm afraid we may not be far from the truth.

Despite these changes, it is still true today that physicians' expectations for healthcare organizations are centered around clinical and operational issues that directly affect their patients and their practice. Most physicians today describe a positive overall relationship with hospitals; however, they indicate a decline in their perception of hospitals in the area of trust, leadership, and communication. With that knowledge, we have chosen to focus our efforts to connect with our medical staff on building those three foundations—trust, leadership, and communication.

We've also discovered that physicians are surprisingly open to and invigorated by programs that address these concerns. Just as our employees exceeded our highest level of expectation when we turned our focus to improving patient care and transforming our culture, our physicians have also responded with enthusiasm to our efforts to engage them. As we have developed programs and services that are of value to our physicians and their patients, we have observed a measurable correlation between those same physicians' satisfaction and yes, even loyalty to our hospital system.

Physicians as a whole are much less engaged with the hospitals where they practice than they have been in the past. In most markets, there appear to be three distinct groups of physicians in terms of their interactions with hospitals. First, there is a core group of hospital-based or hospital-dependent physicians including ER physicians, radiologists, anesthesiologists, and selected surgical subspecialists who are still dependent on the hospital for the majority of their clinical work. In contrast to this group, many other specialists have transitioned away from the hospital such as ENTs, ophthalmologists, and plastic surgeons. Much of what these physicians do is now done in ambulatory service centers or outpatient office settings outside the walls of the hospital. Third, with the advent of hospitalists, many primary care physicians now practice in an ambulatory care setting and spend very little time at the hospital.

What does this mean for physician–hospital relationships? How do we build positive working relationships with people who rarely visit our facilities? Hospital medical staff meetings are attended by fewer and fewer physicians all the time; many hospitals have had such poor attendance that they have stopped holding them altogether. The trend toward providing care away from the hospital not only prevents physicians from becoming familiar with hospital management teams, but it also isolates them from one another.

These are the challenges we put before our Physician Loyalty team as we sought to engage our physicians in our cultural turnaround. In many ways, we have succeeded, largely by using the same strategies that we used with our employees and customers. Specifically, I want to share how we have sought to enhance communication between hospital staff and physicians and among our physicians themselves, how we have used reward and recognition with physicians, how we have worked to provide leadership development opportunities to our medical staff, and how we have applied measurement and accountability tools to encourage physician loyalty.

INCREASED COMMUNICATION

I've always said, "If you've talked to one physician in a multiphysician group, you have communicated with one physician in a multiphysician group." We learned the hard way that you cannot count on them to correctly translate and transmit your message among themselves. Before we could expect our physicians to get on board with our cultural changes, we had to help them understand where we were headed. With this goal, our Physician Loyalty and Communications teams began working together to significantly enhance our communication to this hard-to-reach segment of our constituents.

Just as we did with our employees, we set out to create as broad an array of communication opportunities and tools with our physicians as our team could come up with. Let me share a few of those. Our quarterly newsletter, *Doctors Notes,* covers a broad base of topics that are of interest to our physicians. We encourage physician leaders to participate by writing articles on a variety of subjects. We also incorporate physician issues into another of our communication tools—the *BHC Daily.* Physician awareness is a common theme in the *Daily,* reminding our staff to be conscious of physician issues relating to the hospital. We encourage our employees not to assume that the doctors on their units know what's going on around the hospital, but to actively communicate with them when things are happening.

To align and communicate with this new breed of physicians who spend the majority of their time outside of the hospital, specific staff members have been assigned the task of building and maintaining a personal relationship with these doctors. Our Physician Loyalty team identified "hospital ambassadors" who through years of interaction with our physicians had already gained "backstage passes" to the majority of physician offices. These ambassadors are responsible for keeping our physicians engaged and aware of critical things going on in the hospital. They also provide a channel for physicians to offer feedback as we communicate with them.

Communication is a two-way street, and we wanted our physicians to have ample opportunities to share their concerns, frustrations, and ideas with us. To this end, we have installed a system called *ACT* containing profiles of all of our physician practices. Through this system, a physician can call at any time of day or night to dictate a concern or compliment to our recording system. The very next business day, that call is transcribed and sent to the leader who most closely owns the problem or praise. When the physician has expressed a concern, our leader has 24 hours to respond in writing with an apology and an action plan. The hospital administrator also sends the physician a note to let him know that a leader will be in contact very soon. One month later, the administrator sends a follow-up letter to make sure that the problem was adequately resolved. By empowering our physicians to initiate this process, we increase their satisfaction and improve our service as well.

REWARD AND RECOGNITION

Senior Vice President of Medical Affairs Dr. Craig Miller has worked hard to encourage the recognition of individual physicians. He sends birthday cards to every member of the medical staff, and he regularly provides names of physicians to our administrative staff so that they can write thank-you notes to those who have excelled in demonstrating one of our standards (see Figure A.1). He has challenged us to celebrate the clinical achievements of our medical staff through a variety of media channels. We've even recognized our physicians as Champions and Legends when their contributions merited it.

FIGURE A.1 Thank-You Note to Physician Sample

May 28, 2004

Dear Dr. Leker:

Baptist Hospital strives to provide the best health care to all of our patients. One of the ways we know if we are achieving our goal is to monitor our progress through patient letters and our patient satisfaction surveys.

At the bottom of this page is a comment we received from a recent survey or letter. It gives us great pleasure to know that your patients think so highly of you. Thank you for your continuing support of the mission and vision of Baptist Health Care.

If you have questions or comments, please feel free to contact Medical Affairs at 555-5555. We will be happy to review how we receive these comments and answer any questions you might have.

Sincerely,

Craig Miller, M.D.

"Dr. Leker was very informative. I could not have asked for better care."

In Chapter 8, Celebrating Successes through Reward and Recognition, I listed other ways we use reward and recognition to engage our physicians. The principle of positive reinforcement applies just as readily to physicians as to any other employees. When we acknowledge and reward them for a job well done, they will likely continue those same behaviors (see Figure A.2).

FIGURE A.2 Ways to Recognize Physicians

- Handwritten thank you notes

- Family events

- Doctor's Day luncheons with gifts

- Leadership Retreats (that may include their families)

- Seek their input to facilitate change or process improvement efforts

- New physician orientation

- Physician "mingling" (to welcome and introduce new physicians)

- Newspaper articles

- WOWs

- Press releases

- Letters to physicians who are mentioned in surveys

- Leadership development strategy

- Leaders' pictures in hallways

- Christmas luncheons for physicians and their staff

- Gift certificates to physician leaders (as a Christmas gift)

- Birthday cards from administration

- Cookie baskets to department chairs for their hard work

- Doctors' Notes publication

- Web site recognition

LEADERSHIP DEVELOPMENT

Just as it is not realistic to expect every great floor nurse to have the skills to be a great leader, it is similarly unrealistic to think that every physician elected to a medical staff leadership role has developed the kind of leadership skills to make him or her effective in those roles. Over the years medical staff members have undergone arduous training programs; however, those training programs have historically not led to an atmosphere of collaboration and sharing in a teamwork setting. Years ago I was exposed to a study done in the Northeast that determined that, given a specific team problem, nine out of ten groups of MBA students achieved a win-win solution. Given the same problem, only one out of ten groups of MDs achieved a win-win solution. Why the discrepancy? From the first day of medical school, physicians are taught to be decisive, independent practitioners. That being the case, how can we expect them to move into leadership roles on the medical staff and be effective?

Recognizing this challenge, Dr. Miller stepped outside the box and asked a number of current and future physician leaders if they would like to be a part of a leadership development team and commit an hour a week to learning leadership skills. Every single physician that he asked said yes and when others heard about it, they asked for personal invitations. This team studied leadership books, including *Who Moved My Cheese* by Spencer Johnson (Putnam, 1998), *The Five Dysfunctions of a Team* by Patrick M. Lencioni (Jossey-Bass, 2002), and *Good to Great* by Jim Collins (Harper-Business, 2001), and looked for ways to apply the management principles in these books to today's medical staff. As a result, these physicians gained a better understanding of the collaborative nature of highly functioning teams. They began to understand and embrace our philosophy of open communication, no secrets, and no excuses. As a result, they were able to appreciate the changes within the clinical operations of the hospital and began to take ownership in them.

We now place great emphasis on the educational component of our annual physician leadership retreat, involving them in interactive discussions around the previously taboo area of personal development. This valuable time of reflection and self-assessment for administrative staff and medical leaders from all of our Baptist facilities has been a huge win. We have been overwhelmed by the positive, eager response our physicians have shown for every leadership training opportunity we have offered.

MEASUREMENT AND ACCOUNTABILITY

I can't conclude this section without talking about measurement. A healthy hospital–physician relationship must include tools to measure progress. One such tool for us has been our hospital physician accountability report. This report gives confidential feedback directly to our physicians about many key areas of interest in regard to hospital functions, including patient satisfaction, timeliness of early morning labs, radiology data turnaround, and dictation timeliness. It allows for severity adjusted data to be provided to each of the physicians, with comparison and outcome data such as morbidity, mortality, and complication rates, along with readmission rates. This tool is extremely effective in communicating the opportunities that we all have to improve clinical outcomes and to encourage physician participation and performance improvement planning.

We had an interesting experience in the realm of imposing measurement tools on our physicians when we told our emergency physicians that we were going to base their incentive payments on patient satisfaction scores. They immediately argued, challenging the statistical validity of the scores and offering multiple excuses why this was not appropriate. Eventually we were forced to change physician groups. When the new group realized we were serious, they began looking for ways to deliver better service, and they found them. Dr. Michael Dolister, the group's Medical Director, shared some of the changes they made: "One of the first things we do when we come into a patient room is we sit down. Studies done over 20 years ago show that if a physician sits down and there is no clock in the room, the patient will estimate that the physician is in the room for twice as long if they're sitting versus standing. We have TVs in every room so that when patients are waiting they have something to do. Sometimes we're not able to get patients back in the main emergency department to a room when we would like to, so physicians have developed a mechanism to see patients out of the waiting room in one of the side rooms just adjacent to the waiting room, and that helps facilitate decreased waiting time." These changes might not have come about had we not applied measurement and accountability tools to our ER physicians.

We also use a yearly physician survey tool. Just this year, we transitioned to a nationally-known physician survey instrument so that we could compare ourselves against other organizations and have the opportunity to benchmark. By allowing our medical staff to compare their satisfaction results with more than 500 other hospitals, they can more readily identify opportunities for improvement. This year our results ranged from the seventy-ninth percentile in quality and medical records to the ninety-sixth percentile in quality of radiology and nursing services. We still have work to do; however, our physicians' satisfaction with nursing care echoes what our patients have been telling us for the last eight years. The level of care by our nursing staff is exceptional and much appreciated by our medical staff.

These efforts to engage our physicians—from increased communication to reward and recognition to leadership training to holding them accountable—have certainly contributed to increased physician loyalty. We are living proof that, even as physicians across the country become more and more estranged from the facilities at which they practice, a WOW! culture that contributes to their success can continue to engage physicians in meaningful ways. Ultimately, physicians want to offer excellent care to the patients they serve. When they become convinced that the things we ask of them contribute to that goal, they get on board.

As our cultural change took place, we began to hear stories that let us know that our physicians were "getting it." We heard of physicians who had started walking hospital visitors to their destinations, imitating the "Baptist Behavior" they had seen our employees perform. But I really knew we were getting somewhere when I heard the story of a physician who was leaving the doctor's lounge after a break. As he exited the lounge, fresh cup of coffee in hand, he passed a patient's family in the hall. A member of the family commented, "Mmm. That coffee sure smells good." Immediately the doctor handed his cup to the visitor and said, "Here, take mine. I'll go get another cup."

Giving away cups of coffee is not something we specifically ask our employees—or physicians—to do. It is simply the natural result of building a culture that strives to exceed customer expectations. That physician had seen the power of a WOW! environment, and he chose to become a part of it.

This recent comment from ophthalmologist Dr. Saul Ullman confirms that we are on the right track: "I would not be affiliated with an organization that I didn't think was devoted to patient care and was not on board with having the best employees possible. Treating employees well, having a positive environment—it all affects my patients. I saw a patient today on whom I operated last week who said that she felt like she was taken care of

during the surgery like she was in heaven. That's quite a powerful statement. How good the physician is doesn't matter if the patients don't have
a good feel for the other people—the person that met her when she
checked in, the pre-op nurses, the surgery nurses, the post-op nurses, all of
them. It's all about teamwork, and certainly this organization excels at
patient excellence."

INDEX